The
Lifeskills For Adult Children
Workbook

Janet G. Woititz
and Alan Garner

Health Communications, Inc.
Deerfield Beach, Florida

©1991 Janet G. Woititz and Alan Garner
ISBN 1-55874-130-5

Publisher: Health Communications, Inc.
3201 S.W. 15th Street
Deerfield Beach, Florida 33442-8190

Contents

Introduction

This workbook is the companion to *Lifeskills For Adult Children*. That book made you aware of skills for meeting people and making friends, for getting in touch with your feelings and expressing them, for setting up boundaries and defending them, and for working out your problems with others. That book taught you how to use these skills effectively.

Awareness and knowledge are important, but they won't change your life. Only taking action can do that. This workbook is designed to guide you in moving on to that critical action phase. It includes plenty of exercises to help you practice these skills, experience how they work and begin getting really good at them. It features tips for effectively using your new skills. And it gives you homework assignments designed to get you started using these skills in your everyday life.

If you haven't done so already, we suggest you read *Lifeskills* in full before starting this book. Then, before you do the exercises in each chapter, re-read the corresponding chapter in *Lifeskills*. This workbook focuses only on the skills needed and parts of skills students typically find most challenging. Further, it provides only a capsule summary of them. So to get the complete picture and achieve real mastery of these skills you absolutely will need to study *Lifeskills*.

Take your time in making your way through this book. Promise yourself — in writing — that you will set aside half an hour or an hour each day to practice these skills. And instead of racing through the book all at once, do the exercises and homework in one chapter before moving on to the next. Supplement the exercises by setting up your own "Program for Learning" as described in the Appendix to *Lifeskills*. Consider keeping a "Victory!" notebook to record your successes. (Successes *only* — remember, you grow by building on your strengths, not by focusing on your present weaknesses.) It may take you anywhere from one hour to several weeks per chapter, but whatever it takes, give yourself that time.

The chapters are self-contained. You may decide to change the order and not go from the beginning to the end. The chapter order is designed to have one set of skills lead to the next, but you may want to work them differently. There is no right or wrong way.

Change takes effort, and it absolutely will take effort for you to get good at these skills. *Make that effort.* Do the exercises. Do the homework. The skills may seem difficult at first, but soon you'll find them easier and easier. And after a while you'll find yourself using them automatically, without effort.

Now, as you move into action, we're excited for you. You are soon going to see how learning a few skills can make a big, positive difference in your life.

                                        Janet G. Woititz and Alan Garner

1

Making Contact With Others

Starting Conversations

The Skill:

Making contact by *asking a question about the other person or the situation you are both in.*

Tip: Don't waste time searching for the "perfect" opener. Boring ordinary openers work even better than clever ones. If you still can't think of what to say using this skill, just say something. When you say something — anything — at least you've established contact and have a chance to get a conversation going.

Example

At the library, you notice that the person sitting opposite you is reading *The Flying Boy*. He looks up at you and smiles. You say: *That looks like an interesting book. What's it about?*

1

Exercise

Write out how you would begin a conversation in each of the following situations:

1. At a party you see someone talking to your old friend Nancy.
You say: _____

_____

2. In the park you see someone painting a picture of the water fountain.
You say: _____

_____

3. During a break from your ACoA group, you hear someone say she is taking tennis lessons.
You say: _____

_____

4. Someone shows up at group wearing an "I Like Ike" button.
You say: _____

_____

5. While out for a walk, you spot someone walking a dachshund.
You say: _____

_____

6. Between horse races, you find yourself standing next to someone holding tickets for a horse named Long Shot.
You say: _____

_____

7. In line at the market, you are in front of someone who is purchasing an exotic-looking fruit.

You say: _____

_____

_____

8. In class on the day of an exam, the person next to you smiles.

You say: _____

_____

_____

9. At the laundry you notice someone struggling to fold his sheets all by himself.

You say: _____

_____

_____

10. While out on a hike, you stop at a rest stop. Someone has on a T-shirt which reads "Love Means Letting Go of Fear."

You say: _____

_____

_____

11. At a museum you and another person are standing in front of a huge painting that consists of a white canvas with a red stripe down the center.

You say: _____

_____

_____

12. At the gym you are waiting for someone to finish using a piece of equipment you aren't quite sure how to use correctly.

You say: _____

_____

_____

13. In the wet sauna you and the person next to you are sweating profusely.

You say: _____

_____

_____

14. Sitting at the counter at a diner, you aren't sure what to order. You turn to the person sitting next to you.

You say: _____

_____

_____

15. Before an AA meeting, an interesting-looking woman wearing a bright yellow and blue muumuu sits down next to you.

You say: _____

_____

_____

Practice delivering each of these comments into a tape recorder. As you listen back, ask yourself: "Am I too soft? Too loud?" "Did my voice project an 'I'm OK — You're OK' image?" "Was my voice flat or lively?" Next tape yourself again, taking these comments into account and experimenting with various changes in pitch and loudness. Continue repeating this process until you are happy with your verbal delivery.

Practice delivering each of these comments while facing a mirror. Ask yourself if your facial expressions and the rest of your body language appear welcoming or distancing. Adjust your delivery accordingly as you repeat this exercise until you are satisfied with this nonverbal aspect of your delivery.

Homework

Once a day for the next month, begin a conversation with an acquaintance or a stranger. Use the other skills in *Lifeskills* to help keep these conversations going. Compliment yourself for making the effort regardless of the outcome. If you feel especially anxious about beginning a conversation with someone, promise yourself a reward for doing it, no matter what happens. A reward can be anything you want and would enjoy. Watching a video you have been wanting to see, taking a brisk walk or buying a shirt you've admired are examples of rewards you might give yourself.

Asking Open Questions

The Skill:

Asking questions that require more than just a one or two word answer. Open questions normally being with *"How,"* *"Why,"* or *"Tell me about,"* and sometimes with *"What."*

Tip: Beware of asking questions that are too open, that ask for too much information. And if you don't yet know enough about the other person to ask an open question, begin with a closed question that asks for specific information. Also, getting started may sometimes be easier if you begin with an "I" statement. For instance, in the following example your first words might be, "I've always wanted to go to Australia."

Example

George: I just got back from Australia.
Closed question: *How long were you there?*
Open question: *What was the highlight of your trip?*

Exercise

Various conversational partners you meet during the course of an evening make each of the following statements. Write down one closed question and two open questions that you might ask in response.

1. I'm a high school teacher.

Closed question: _____

_____

Open question 1: _____

_____

Open question 2: _____

_____

2. I have a twin sister back in Minnesota.

Closed question: _____

_____

Open question 1: _____

_____

Open question 2: _____

_____

3. I just signed up to be a Big Sister.

Closed question: _____

_____

Open question 1: _____

_____

Open question 2: _____

_____

4. Everyone says a college education is important. I disagree.

Closed question: _____

_____

Open question 1: _____

_____

Open question 2: _____

_____

5. I've decided to return to school to finish up my counseling degree.

Closed question: _____

_____

Open question 1: _____

_____

Open question 2: _____

_____

6. I'm having a dickens of a time finding a new house I can afford to buy.

Closed question: _____

_____

Open question 1: _____

_____

Open question 2: _____

_____

7. I don't think the people who run this country really care about cleaning up the environment.

Closed question: _____

_____

Open question 1: _____

_____

Open question 2: _____

_____

8. It looks like another dry year.

Closed question: _____

_____

Open question 1: _____

_____

Open question 2: _____

_____

9. I'm not sure where to vacation this year, but the only place I know I'm *not* going is Paris.

Closed question: _____

_____

Open question 1: _____

_____

Open question 2: _____

_____

10. The little guy like me just doesn't stand a chance in the stock market anymore.

Closed question: _____

_____

Open question 1: _____

_____

Open question 2: _____

_____

11. I dread going home for the holidays.

Closed question: _____

_____

Open question 1: _____

_____

Open question 2: _____

_____

12. I always feel I should be able to handle my problems by myself.

Closed question: _____

_____

Open question 1: _____

_____

Open question 2: _____

_____

13. I just read *I Don't Want To Be Alone,* and I really find myself identifying with the author.

Closed question: _____

_____

Open question 1: _____

_____

Open question 2: _____

_____

14. I got rolfed yesterday. Boy, is that painful!

Closed question: _____

_____

Open question 1: _____

_____

Open question 2: _____

_____

15. I've just been listening to Janet Woititz's tape *Adult Children of Alcoholics.*

Closed question: _____

_____

Open question 1: _____

_____

Open question 2: _____

_____

Practice delivering each of the comments above while talking into a tape recorder and facing a mirror. Ask yourself what you liked about your delivery and what could be better. Continue practicing until you are happy with your delivery. Be sure to compliment yourself for what you did well.

Exercise

Find a partner. Each of you write down three things about yourself that you are willing to share. For example, the last book you have read, a good movie you've seen recently, the place you went on your last vacation, the place you grew up, any hobbies you have and what you do for a living. Next, exchange pieces of paper. You begin by asking an open question about one fact written on the other person's piece of paper. The other person responds in 20 or 30 seconds and then asks you an open question. Continue asking each other open questions for five or six minutes. If need be, either of you can ask a closed question or two — and then follow up with an open question. If either of you is asked closed or too-open questions, respond with one- or two-word answers. In that way you will train each other to ask only open questions.

Exercise

Find a partner. Each of you write down three different things about yourself. Take your partner's piece of paper and keep your own. Keep your partner talking for five minutes by asking mostly open questions, both about subjects that are written down and as follow-ups to things that are said. Then switch roles.

Picking Up On Conversational Cues

The Skill:

When you ask questions, others will frequently give you more information than you requested. Following up on conversational cues means *making comments* or *asking questions* (preferably open questions) about this extra information. Other conversational clues you can pick up on include others' clothes, jewelry, accents and books.

Tip: Don't worry about getting too personal. When someone drops a conversational cue, 99 percent of the time they want you to ask about it. They have opened the door hoping you will enter. So if the topic interests you too, go for it!

> ### Example
>
> You: <u>Terry, you look like you've lost ten pounds!</u>
> Terry: Thanks. *I quit dieting and started an exercise program.*
> You: <u>What made you decide to do that?</u>

Exercise

Write out how you would follow up on each of these conversational cues:

1. You: Great-looking pearls, Pat. They just shine!
Pat: Thanks. *Rob and I got them at a pearl factory in Majorca.*

You: _____

_____

2. You: Good speech, Margie! You seemed so sure of yourself.
Margie: Thanks. *I used to get nervous speaking, but I don't anymore.*

You: _____

_____

3. You: This table looks terrific, Kelly! The marble just glows.
Kelly: It does, doesn't it. *The stonecutter let us pick out the piece before he made the table.*

You: _____

_____

4. You: I notice you have a foreign accent. Where are you from?
Walt: England. *Doctors there can hardly make a living, so I came over here to practice.*

You: _____

_____

5. You: Here it is mid-summer, and you're white as a sheet.
Deborah: Yeah, *I'm taking all that talk about the sun aging skin seriously. So I've been using a sun block.*

You: _____

_____

6. You: I notice you've got a Rutger's T-shirt on. Are you from there?

Jack: *No, I just went there one summer. But I loved that school so much, I still like wearing this old T-shirt.*

You: _____

_____

7. You: Did you and Patty just meet?

Amy: No, *we went to boarding school together when we were kids.*

You: _____

_____

8. You: Looks like it's starting to rain.

Andy: This is nothing. *You should have seen it where I grew up in Kansas!*

You: _____

_____

9. You: Congratulations on your new car!

Sally: Thanks, *it was really hard for me to become successful in sales, but I did it!*

You: _____

_____

10. You: Hey, new hat?

Barbara: Yeah, *I bought it to celebrate my divorce!*

You: _____

_____

Practice delivering each of these comments into a tape recorder and while facing a full-length mirror. Repeat until you are happy with your delivery.

Exercise

Find a partner and ask a question to get things rolling. Be on the lookout for conversational cues, and when you find them, follow up with still more questions about them. Your goal is to keep the other person talking for five minutes by following up on one conversational cue after another.

Using Dual Perspective

The Skill:

Thinking not just in terms of what you would like to say, but also *in terms of what the other person is likely to enjoy talking about*. To use Dual Perspective, start by asking yourself, "What is this person likely to be interested in discussing?" If nothing comes to mind, put yourself in his or her place and ask yourself, "What would I be interested in talking about in this situation?"

Example

A friend says, "I've decided to attend the National ACoA Conference in Orlando."

Using Dual Perspective, write out three things you could say:

1. *Why did you decide to attend?*
2. *What's the biggest thing you hope to get out of the conference?*
3. *Great! I've found attending conferences is a great way to meet people I can relate to — and learn at the same time.*

Exercise

Write out three questions or comments you could make, using Dual Perspective, in response to each of the following statements from a close friend. Resist the temptation to give advice.

You know, I'm just not happy anymore on my job.

1: _____

2: _____

3: _____

I've thought about it a lot, and I'm filing for divorce.

1: _____

2: _____

3: _____

I'm tired of worrying about my mortgage. I think I'm going to find some little place in the country.

1: _____

2: _____

3: _____

I just had my 40th birthday, and I looked around at my husband and my kids and my job, and I decided I'm really happy with how things are.

1: _____

2: _____

3: _____

I just read *The Doormat Syndrome*, and I think the author could have been writing about me.

1: _____

2: _____

3: _____

I've decided to visit Disney World this Christmas.

1: _____

2: _____

3: _____

I've started my 29th diet.

1: _____

2: _____

3: _____

I think I was happier about my life when I was in denial.

1: _____

2: _____

3: _____

I've decided to go back to school to study counseling.

1: _____

2: _____

3: _____

My doctor told me I don't need to take vitamins, but I don't agree.

1: _____

2: _____

3: _____

Get Specific

The Skill:

Giving *details* of *the highlights* of what you saw, heard and felt. What you say will tend to be interesting when you talk in specifics and boring when you talk in general terms.

Tip: Don't try to summarize everything. If you do, your talk will end up being general — and boring. Instead, begin by saying "One time . . ." and then relating the highlight.

Example

General: My cruise had lots of terrific food.
Specific: The first day I gorged myself — top sirloin steak, duck a l'orange, coq au vin, salmon! . . . After all, it was free, I told myself. But that night I had a massive and very painful stomachache, and I regretted every bite I had taken.

Exercise

Make the following general statements specific.

1. Marie treated me okay. _____

_____

_____

2. I had fun in Atlantic City. _____

_____

_____

3. He was scarey looking. _____

_____

_____

4. It's a good book. _____

_____

_____

5. He was nice. _____

_____

_____

6. The sale was easy! _____

_____

_____

7. The house looked beautiful. _____

_____

_____

8. The show was entertaining. _____

_____

_____

9. It was a good speech. _____

_____

_____

10. This exercise is hard. _____

_____

_____

Sharing Yourself

The Skill:

Using the word "I" and *telling how you relate* to the specifics you talk about. This means sharing facts, opinions and feelings about yourself. In the following example, consider how much better you relate to this bank teller because he is specific and shares himself.

Example

"I'm a bank teller and sometimes I feel that people think I'm not flesh and blood, that I'm the automatic teller. I used to have a gal who came to my line. I thought she liked me, so I said to her one time, 'Say, when are you going for lunch?' She looked up and said to me, 'I'll take that in twenties please.' My blood ran cold and I felt so depressed. I wondered how my life ever came to that."

Exercise

Add something to the following statements to show ownership of the ideas by starting the next sentence with the word "I."

1. It was difficult.

I _____

_____

2. It was entertaining.

I _____

_____

3. You would have liked it.

I _____

_____

4. What an incredible show!

I _____

_____

5. It was discouraging.

I _____

_____

6. You never had a chance.

I _____

_____

7. You couldn't see ten feet ahead.

I _____

_____

8. It was hard reading.

I _____

_____

9. You should have seen it!

I _____

_____

10. It was memorable.

I _____

_____

Exercise

People often try to disguise ownership of their thoughts and feelings by asking questions instead of making statements. Change the following questions into thoughts, beginning with the word "I."

1. Sure you don't want to go?

I _____

_____

2. How about taking in a movie?

I _____

_____

3. Aren't you tired?

I _____

_____

4. Isn't service here awful?

I _____

_____

5. Isn't that book hard?

I _____

_____

6. Don't you think that's sad?

I _____

_____

7. Isn't this food a bit pricey?

I _____

_____

8. Wouldn't it be great to just take off and run away to Europe?

I _____

_____

9. Isn't *When Harry Met Sally* the funniest movie?

I _____

_____

10. Wouldn't you rather go somewhere quieter?

I _____

_____

Exercise

Find a partner. Tell your partner about how you relate to the first subject listed below, sharing at least one related *fact* about yourself and one personal *opinion*. The other person then does the same for the first topic. Next, you address the second topic, and so forth.

school busing
ACoA groups
taking risks
income tax
cars
dieting
exercising
relaxing
cooking
pollution
men
spending money

Exercise

Find a partner and answer the first of the questions below, making a special effort to *share yourself* and *be specific*. You can share yourself by relating personal *facts, opinions* and *feelings*. You can be specific by answering questions as though they were open, even when they are too open or closed.

For example, if you answer Question One below by saying, "I'm from Kansas City and had many interesting experiences growing up there," that'll be boring. Better to focus on *one* interesting experience you had growing up in Kansas City. One way to do this is to begin relating the experience by saying the words, "One time . . ." and telling a brief story focusing on a highlight. After you have answered the first question, the other person gets a turn answering it, then you go on to answer the second question.

1. Where are you from? What was it like growing up there?
2. What is the luckiest thing that ever happened to you?
3. What's the most dangerous thing that ever happened to you?
4. What did you do last night?
5. Tell me about one time when you've used these lifeskills.
6. What was the highlight of your last vacation?
7. Tell me about your greatest social success.
8. Tell me about one time when everything went wrong socially.
9. What's the best buy you ever made?
10. What's your favorite song and why?
11. What do you like best about yourself?
12. How have you liked the exercises in this book so far?

Homework

Find an acquaintance and mentally rate how you feel about that person right now, with "1" meaning you hate them and "10" meaning you like them tremendously. Spend at least five minutes letting that person get to know you and getting to know them, and then make a second rating. Chances are your second rating is several points higher than the first. (By the way, chances are that his or her rating of you has gone up too!) Note how this person, who perhaps started off as just a face in the crowd, has now become much more in your mind, maybe even someone you'd like to become friends with.

Homework

Do the following exercise two times each week for the next two months: Write the names of two acquaintances you will speak with this week and two topics you and they might well be interested in discussing. For example:

1. Dan — stamps, telescopes
2. Andi — cooking, travel

When you see those people, start a conversation and bring up one or both of your topics. Use the conversational skills in this chapter. Your goal is to keep the conversation going for at least five minutes. Each time you achieve your goal, remember to compliment yourself and give yourself a reward.

2

Expressing Feelings

Identifying Your Feelings

The Skill:

Focusing your attention on your feelings and becoming aware of them.

Exercise

Pay attention to your feelings in your daily life. Begin by setting aside a minute or two every half-hour for a week to focus on whatever *physical sensations* you may be experiencing from the outside world, such as touch, temperature and smell. For example, when you take your morning shower, focus on the soothing warmth of the water, on the feel of the water bouncing off your skin. Then when you eat breakfast, take time to smell it and to experience the texture and the cold or warmth of the food as you eat it.

The next week, focus on *nonthreatening feelings* your body is generating. For example, when you wake up, pay attention to how you feel. You might be ready to name how you feel (groggy, happy, headachy) or you might not. And each half-hour, focus for one or two minutes on experiencing these feelings. (Our thanks to San Diego therapist Beverly Hershfield for suggesting this exercise.)

Name Your Feeling

The Skill:

Summarizing your feelings in a word.

Exercise

For one week, spend a moment or two every half-hour paying attention to your feelings. If you are ready, allow yourself to experience physical sensations, nonthreatening feelings and all other feelings. At this point, having become used to feelings, you'll find that feelings of anger and fear won't have quite the impact they once had. And they'll have even less impact when you take the next step, which is to name them and write them down. If you have problems naming your feelings at first, name which of the four basic feelings — sad, mad, glad and scared — you are experiencing. Then work on identifying shades of feeling.

The following format may prove a good way to organize your list of feelings.

On waking up, I feel _____

_____

In the shower, I feel _____

_____

At breakfast, I feel _____

_____

Going to work, I feel _____

_____

Expressing Positive Feeling/Complimenting

The Skill:

Being specific about exactly what it is you liked, *saying the person's name* and *following up with a question.*

Homework

For the next week, set a goal of identifying ten things each day that you appreciate about others' behavior, appearance and possessions. Complete the first day's list below:

Things I Liked

1. _____
2. _____
3. _____
4. _____
5. _____
6. _____
7. _____
8. _____
9. _____
10. _____

After you have become good at identifying compliment opportunities, set a goal of delivering one compliment each day for the following week, then two a day for the week after that and three a day for the week after that. If you have a date book, use it to keep track of your progress.

Saying "I Love You"

The Skill:

Telling someone directly that you love them.

Homework

Saying "I love you" to someone is sometimes easiest if you work up to it step by step. Begin by including it parenthetically in a note. Write, for example, "Since I love you, I want to be sure you're safe . . ." You've made the point but not really taken much of a risk. Next, begin closing your letters to that person with "Love" or "I love you." Then tell the person you love them in the same way you wrote them. Then, perhaps just as you are leaving, call out, "See you later. I love you." That way you won't have to worry about being around for the response. By that time there may well have been some open response to your words, and even if there's not, at this juncture you may be ready to say it openly. Or you may be happy with having made your point and may not choose to go further with it.

Expressing Negative Feelings

The Skill:

Being *clear* and *direct* about what you don't like and *how you feel about it*.

Tip: Speak up about minor irritations as they happen. Otherwise your pent-up feelings will build up and you may someday explode with anger. Begin your feeling statements with the word "I" ("I feel angry . . .") in order to acknowledge that you are ultimately responsible for your feelings. Statements beginning with "You" ("You make me mad") blame the other person for how you feel and give away your personal power over your feelings.

Example

A friend borrows a book and hasn't returned it in two months. You say: I'm upset that you haven't returned my book yet.

Exercise

In each of the following situations, write out how you would express your negative feelings. Be sure to *be clear and direct* and to *own your own feelings* by beginning your feeling statements with "I" rather than "You."

1. A friend walks in and gets mud on your carpet.

_____

_____

_____

2. A friend promised to call you back in half an hour and is calling now — an hour later.

_____

_____

_____

3. A child smudges your white walls with his dirty hands.

_____

_____

_____

4. A friend is returning your car — three hours late.

_____

_____

_____

5. A friend is an hour late picking you up and didn't call to let you know she was delayed.

_____

_____

_____

6. A friend you had planned to go out with cancels at the last minute without a reason.

_____

_____

_____

7. A neighbor tells your relatives of your failed attempts to be your own gardener.

_____

_____

_____

8. A child lied to you about having no homework to do.

_____

_____

_____

9. A friend said she'd introduce you to her brother a month ago and still hasn't.

_____

_____

_____

10. A child's pounding with his hammer is annoying you.

_____

_____

_____

Record yourself on tape delivering each of the comments above. When you play it back, ask yourself: "Was I too loud? Too soft?" "Did my tone of voice match what I was saying?" "How else might I improve my delivery?" Make another recording and listen again to see where you improved and how you could do better. Continue until you are satisfied with your delivery.

Find a partner and role-play delivering each of the comments above. Ask your friend to tell you what you do well and how you could do even better. Practice until you are satisfied with your delivery.

Homework

When you become upset with someone, express your negative feelings in writing. Then, when you feel comfortable doing so, begin speaking up about minor irritations. Always be sure to compliment yourself on your efforts.

3

Active Listening

Becoming An Active Listener

The Skill:

Putting into your own words your understanding of what the other person is saying. As you listen, ask yourself, *"What is this person feeling?"* and *"What is this person saying?"* Depending on whether you think the emotion or the content is most important, share your answer to the appropriate question. This is your active listening statement. If you are correct, the other person will usually tell you so and will expand on what he said originally. If you are wrong, the other person will most likely correct you. Either way, using active listening will enable you to be certain you understood what the other person said and will encourage that person to talk on.

Tip: Resist the temptation to rush in with solutions to other people's problems. Most often they don't want your advice; they simply want to know you heard them. There will be no doubt about that when you use active listening.

Example

Husband: It looks like I'm not gonna get that raise.
Wife: You feel frustrated.
Husband: I am. I've been working on this sale for months, and I've come so close.
Wife: *You've just about had it.*
Husband: And now somebody's coming in offering them a better deal.
Wife: *You feel you've spent a lot of time and you're getting nothing for it.*

Exercise

You can use Active Listening to reflect back the *emotion* or the *content* of what the other person is saying. Practice responding to the following statements by doing both. Remember, there is no "perfect" answer. Even guesses about emotion or content that turn out not to be accurate are valuable as they encourage the other person to speak up and lead to understanding.

1. Steven: My check from Jack didn't come again today.

You (emotion): You sound angry.

You (content): Jack still hasn't paid you.

2. Dorothy: Earl stood me up.

You (emotion): _____

You (content): _____

3. Erick: I've got a test tomorrow and I'm just not prepared at all!

You (emotion): _____

You (content): _____

4. Sandy: I got a speeding ticket today.

You (emotion): _____

You (content): _____

5. Gene: It's all set — Randi and I are going to Europe!

You (emotion): _____

You (content): _____

6. Ron: My sister's coming to live with me.

You (emotion): _____

You (content): _____

7. Art: I'm retiring from 3M next year.

You (emotion): _____

You (content): _____

8. Donna: It's too cold here. I think I'd like to move to Florida.

You (emotion): _____

You (content): _____

9. Manny: I don't like John's sense of humor — the way he's always putting me down.

You (emotion): _____

You (content): _____

10. Anna: My husband never talks to me anymore.

You (emotion): _____

You (content): _____

11. Gretchen: Seventeen is *not* too young to go on a date!

You (emotion): _____

You (content): _____

12. Mike: I got the raise!

You (emotion): _____

You (content): _____

13. Melanie: Doug finally asked me out!

You (emotion): _____

You (content): _____

14. Tom: I would give anything to move back to Austin.

You (emotion): _____

You (content): _____

15. Lynn: All he does is come home and watch TV.

You (emotion): _____

You (content): _____

Exercise

Use Active Listening to fill in the blank spaces in these dialogues.

1. Ellie: I'm mad at Michael.

You: _____

_____

_____

Ellie: Yeah. He wouldn't let me play with his friends.

You: _____

_____

_____

Ellie: Right, and I had nobody to play with.

2. Joe: I got turned down for that new job.

You: _____

_____

_____

Joe: I am. I'll never get ahead. I'll never amount to anything.

You: _____

_____

_____

3. Morrie: They loved me tonight! I've never had applause like that!

You: _____

_____

_____

Morrie: Yes, and it felt terrific! All my study and practice, it was all worth it tonight!

You: _____

_____

_____

4. April (drooping): My Step Study? Oh, it was fine, I guess.

You: _____

_____

_____

April: No, it's just that I wanted to go up and speak, but I didn't.

You: _____

_____

_____

April: Right. So I just sat there and got depressed.

You: _____

_____

_____

5. Doris: I wish we'd never come to the Virgin Islands.

You: _____

_____

_____

Doris: You got that right. Everything is *so expensive* — it's like our dollars are worth nothing!

You: _____

_____

_____

Doris: The taxi drivers charge us *per person*.

You: _____

_____

_____

Doris: Nobody's friendly . . . Everybody's got their hand out . . .

You: _____

_____

_____

Doris: Right. It would have been more fun if we'd stayed home — and $3,000 cheaper!

You: _____

_____

_____

Doris: For the same money, let's go to Greece next year. At least the Greeks genuinely like Americans.

You: _____

_____

_____

6. Emily: Do you want to stay 'til the end of the movie?

You: _____

_____

_____

Emily: Right. I'm getting a headache.

You: _____

_____

_____

Emily: Yes. (Now outside the theater) Movies like this . . . Well, I thought *Teenage Mutant Ninja Turtles* would be a nice little cartoon about turtles playing with each other.

You: _____

_____

_____

Emily: Right. But there's more fighting and killing than in ten ordinary movies. I felt like I was watching *The Terminator!*

You: _____

_____

_____

Emily: In my day, they didn't have movies like this.

You: _____

_____

_____

Emily: That's true. They had wholesome movies like *Top Hat* and *Adam's Rib.*

You: _____

_____

_____

Emily: Exactly.

You: _____

_____

_____

7. Paulette: I'm not sure what I want to do with my life.

You: _____

_____

_____

Paulette: You got it. Teaching sounds like fun, but they don't pay teachers anything.

You: _____

_____

_____

Paulette: Right. But I do like the idea of three months off.

You: _____

_____

_____

Paulette: Yeah . . . And I know business is where the big money is, but I don't think I'm cut out for it.

You: _____

_____

_____

Paulette: Right. I don't like acting so serious all the time. I'd rather have a job where I can work with kids and laugh a lot.

You: _____

_____

_____

Paulette: Right. And I plan on staying home a few years when I have children, and that's a lot easier to arrange in teaching than in business. In business, you more or less just have to quit.

You: _____

_____

_____

8. Rachael: I'm mad at my fiancee, Howard.

You: _____

_____

_____

Rachael: Yeah, every time we have a fight, he tells me, "You're not educated, so what good is your opinion?"

You: _____

_____

_____

Rachael: I may not have been to college, but I'm just as smart as he is.

You: _____

_____

_____

Rachael: And besides, many of the most successful people haven't been to college.

You: _____

_____

_____

Rachael: You know, when he talks to me like that, I ask myself, "If he feels I'm so dumb, why does he want to marry me anyway?"

You: _____

_____

_____

9. Lillie: Last night I felt really sad.

You: _____

_____

_____

Lillie: Yeah, I was thinking about this boy I used to date and all the fun we used to have.

You: _____

_____

_____

Lillie: Yes, I was kind of missing him. And kind of wishing things had worked out. And wishing I had someone special like him around now.

You: _____

_____

_____

Lillie: Right. I know lots of guys, but I'm kind of picky. I just don't like that many.

You: _____

_____

_____

Lillie: And the ones I do like are usually taken.

You: _____

_____

_____

10. Victoria: I'm not sure if I want to have kids.

You: _____

_____

_____

Victoria: Yes. I hear they keep you awake the first six months.

You: _____

_____

_____

Victoria: And you never regain your figure after you have them. At least my mother never did.

You: _____

_____

_____

Victoria: And they cost all kinds of money. It's $5,000 just for the hospital! And then there are clothes to get and toys and babysitters and bikes . . .

You: _____

_____

_____

Victoria: And I'm not sure what kind of mother I'd be. I mean, I hope I'd be a whole lot more patient than my mother was with me.

You: _____

_____

_____

Victoria: That's true. You know, sometimes I think I'd like to have kids just to do it right. Just to somehow make up for the abuse I had when I was a kid.

You: _____

_____

_____

Victoria: Yeah, not a very good reason, is it.

You: _____

_____

_____

Exercise

Find a partner and have that person answer the first question below, while you use Active Listening to reflect what she says. Go back and forth as long as you like. When you are done, you answer the first question while the other person uses Active Listening. Repeat these instructions with the second and subsequent questions.

1. What is the most important thing you want to accomplish in your life and why?
2. What's the best advice you have ever received? Why was it the best?
3. Who has been the most important person in your life and why?
4. What is your favorite thing to do in your spare time?
5. If you knew you were going to die tomorrow, what would you do today? What would you say?

6. If you knew you were going to die in a year, how would you change your life?
7. What or who do you love the most?
8. What do you fear the most?
9. Tell me about your favorite vacation.
10. Tell me about the greatest challenge you face in your life now.
11. What has been the happiest time in your life?
12. If someone were to write your epitaph, what would it say?
13. How do you see your life being different in five years?
14. If you could live your life over again, what one thing would you do differently?
15. What is the most important lesson you have learned lately? Why is it so important?

4

Asking For What You Want

Figuring Out What You Want

The Skill:

Paying attention to your self-talk and feelings in order to get in touch with what you want. Use this skill when you are unclear or only vaguely clear as to what it is you want.

Tip: To keep track of your self-talk and feelings, carry a piece of paper and write them down.

Exercise

Imagine yourself in each of the following situations. Write down your self-talk and any feelings you have.

1. An important client calls up to invite you to go fishing.

Self-talk: _____

_____

_____

Feelings: _____

_____

2. A friend you're visiting says, "Excuse me for a minute, I want to catch the stock report." He turns on the TV, listens to the stock report and watches another 30 minutes — all the time totally ignoring you.

Self-talk: _____

_____

_____

Feelings: _____

_____

3. You're out driving with a friend when he suddenly says, "Hey, let's go to Sally's! It's only two hours away, and they have great seafood!" Without waiting for your response, your friend turns right and begins driving to Sally's.

Self-talk: _____

_____

_____

Feelings: _____

_____

4. You're trying to read an important article, and your neighbor has his stereo blasting away.

Self-talk: _____

_____

_____

Feelings: _____

_____

5. You're waiting on a busy street corner for a friend who so far is an hour late.

Self-talk: _____

_____

_____

Feelings: _____

_____

6. Five minutes before quitting time, your boss comes up to you with two hours of work he wants you to do right away.

Self-talk: _____

_____

_____

Feelings: _____

_____

7. At a dance your date starts dancing with someone else. Now it's the _third_ song, and they're _still dancing!_

Self-talk: _____

_____

_____

Feelings: _____

_____

8. You and a friend have been driving for five hours nonstop.

Self-talk: _____

_____

_____

Feelings: _____

_____

9. You lend your place to a friend and return home to find it a mess. Newspapers, potato chips, empty soda cups and all sorts of other junk are everywhere!

Self-talk: _____

_____

Feelings: _____

10. You discover that one of your best friends is getting married and hasn't invited you. While you sit home, all your friends are excitedly getting ready for the big event.

Self-talk: _____

_____

_____

Feelings: _____

Homework

Carry a pen and paper with you. When you find things aren't going your way, write down the situation, your self-talk and what you are feeling. At the end of the day, look at what you have written and think of how others might help make things easier and what you might say to ask for their help. Then ask for their help.

Making Requests

The Skill:

Asking for what you want by . . .

Using Dual Perspective: Can they help you? Are they likely to be interested?

Being direct: "Will you listen to my speech and give me your opinion?"

Giving your reason: "Will you please baby-sit tonight? There's a speaker in town I want to go hear."

Appealing to other's self-interest: "If you'll drive me to the airport, I promise to drive you next time you need a ride."

Exercise

For each of the ten instances in the last exercise above, write out a request you might make that could help you in your situation.

1. _____

_____

_____

2. _____

_____

_____

3. _____

_____

_____

4. _____

_____

_____

5. _____

_____

_____

6. _____

_____

_____

7. _____

_____

_____

8. _____

_____

_____

9. _____

_____

_____

10. _____

_____

_____

Practice making the requests above into a tape recorder and in front of a mirror. Continue practicing until you are satisfied with your performance.

Practice reciting the requests to a friend. Ask your friend for positive and then negative feedback.

Exercise

Write out what you would say to make each of the following requests:

1. Ask a co-worker to help you with a report.

_____

_____

2. Ask a family member to help you with yard work.

_____

_____

3. Ask a house guest to help you do the dishes tonight.

_____

_____

4. Ask a friend to pick you up at the airport.

_____

_____

5. Ask a fellow club member to take over your job as treasurer.

_____

_____

6. Ask a co-worker to pick up a sandwich for you.

_____

_____

7. Ask to borrow a friend's copy of *Adult Children of Alcoholics*.

_____

_____

8. Your car won't start. Ask a neighbor to drive you to work.

_____

_____

9. It's three days until payday and you're short. Ask a friend to lend you $50.

_____

_____

10. Ask a friend to listen to a problem.

_____

_____

Practice making each of these requests in front of a mirror and into a tape recorder. Continue practicing until you are satisfied with your delivery.

Role-play making each of these requests with a friend. Ask your friend to tell you what you did well and what you could do even better. Practice until you are satisfied.

Issuing Invitations

The Skill:

Starting small and *sounding casual* as you ask someone to join you.

Tip: Most invitations are accepted. If you act as though acceptance of yours is likely, your positive attitude will make those yeses even more probable.

Exercise

Write out what you might say to issue each of the following invitations:

1. Invite a neighbor over for a barbecue.

_____

_____

2. Invite your boss to lunch.

_____

_____

3. Invite a friend to come over and watch *Wonder Years*.

_____

_____

4. Invite a neighbor you see outside to go for a walk with you.

_____

_____

5. Invite your next-door neighbor over for coffee or tea.

_____

_____

6. Invite a co-worker and his wife to come by your place Friday evening.

_____

_____

7. Invite an acquaintance to go shopping with you.

_____

_____

8. Invite a family member to stay at your place over the weekend.

_____

_____

9. Invite an old friend to bring his family and join you for a picnic.

_____

_____

10. Invite an acquaintance to drop by and show you pictures of her vacation in Italy.

_____

_____

Vividly imagine yourself calmly and confidently issuing each of the above invitations and each time being told "Yes."

Practice issuing each of these invitations while talking into a tape recorder and facing a mirror. Listen to the tape and ask yourself what you did well and how you might do even better. Practice again and again, taking this feedback into account.

Practice issuing each of these invitations to a friend. Tell your friend to say "Yes" each time to your invitation. Ask your friend what you did well and how you might do even better. If you are not sure how to do better, ask your friend to show you. Practice until you are satisfied, each time taking this feedback into account.

Homework

Write down the names of five people you'd like to get to know or spend more time with. Remember to _start small_ as you write out an invitation you might make to each. Looking over the list, find the one about which you feel least anxious. Remember to _sound casual_ as you imagine yourself issuing that invitation and getting a "Yes." Next, practice issuing that invitation alone and to a partner. Then actually do issue that invitation in real life.

Then pick out the second least anxiety-producing invitation and follow the same procedure. Continue until you have issued all five invitations. Be sure to congratulate yourself each time. No matter the response, your efforts will put you firmly on the road to success.

5

Giving Others What They Want

How To Give Others What They Want

The Skills:

Giving others what *they* need or want without trying to manipulate them.

Tip: Don't assume that they want what you want. You're more likely to be correct if you use *Dual Perspective* and ask yourself, "Based on what I know of them, what are they likely to need or want?"

Homework

Over the next week, closely observe and listen to the people you interact with. Look for clues and use *Dual Perspective* to list some things each of them is likely to need or want. The following week, set a goal of giving one person each day something they want. Regardless of the response, be sure to compliment yourself for your efforts.

Exercise

Write down five ways you could give yourself to others (your time, expressions of love and appreciation, encouragement and assistance). Set specific goals for doing so, including a time frame in which you will achieve each goal.

Example

I will give flowers to my sweetheart no later than this Friday.

6

Solving Problems

Deciding Whether A Problem Is Yours

The Skill:

Separating your own problems from other people's problems. A problem is yours when *you* are the person whose needs and desires are not being met.

Exercise

Seven of the following are examples of problems that belong to you and eight are examples of problems that belong to other people. Circle the examples in which the problems belong to other people.

1. A friend is short of cash until payday.
2. A close neighbor is behind on his mortgage payments.
3. Your television set isn't working.
4. Your cousin is having arguments with her husband.

5. A friend forgets to pick you up at work.
6. A television minister needs money to stay on the air.
7. The neighbors' fighting keeps you awake.
8. Your office made a mistake and withheld too much of your pay for taxes.
9. Your best friend is having an emotional crisis.
10. You haven't had time to exercise all week.
11. A good friend needs the help you feel your ACoA group can provide.
12. A fellow you grew up with is in trouble with his boss.
13. You can't afford the down-payment for a house.
14. A boy tells you he needs your newspaper subscription to win a trip to camp.
15. You are late to an important meeting because of a traffic jam.

Answer: Problems 3, 5, 7, 8, 10, 13 and 15 belong to you. Problems 1, 2, 4, 6, 9, 11, 12 and 14 belong to other people. Being able to distinguish between what is your problem and what is not your problem centers your thinking. You may *choose*, for example, to help fund the minister in number six or the friend in crisis in number nine; that choice does not make their problem yours.

Defining Problems In Terms Of
Needs, Not Solutions

The Skill:

Looking behind proposed solutions to discover the *needs* you and others hope to satisfy with those solutions. Ask yourself, "Why do I want this solution?" or "Why do they want that solution?" The answer may well tell you the needs involved. Needs are your requirements in situations; solutions are how you try to satisfy those needs. We all get stuck on solutions that don't work or conflict with others' solutions. If we focus instead on our needs and the needs of others, we could find dozens of often better solutions that would satisfy everyone's needs.

Example

You want to go to an art exhibit; a friend wants to go to a motorcycle race. When you ask yourselves the questions above, you discover both of you feel a need for *entertainment* and neither of you is committed to the solution you proposed to get that need satisfied. Knowing this, you might compromise and decide to take in a play.

Exercise

Suppose you or someone else came up with each of the following solutions. Write down one or more *needs* that solution might fulfill.

1. "We should move to the countryside."

_____

_____

_____

2. "I'm going to quit my job and become a painter."

_____

_____

_____

3. "Let's take a trip around Europe this year."

_____

_____

_____

4. "I think we should volunteer for Big Sisters."

_____

_____

_____

5. "Let's get a brand new car!"

_____

_____

_____

6. "I want a new suit."

_____

_____

_____

7. "Let's rent _Back to the Future III_."

_____

_____

_____

8. "I want to go to the Northeast ACoA Conference."

_____

_____

_____

9. "I think I'll go back to college."

_____

_____

_____

10. "Let's open a Postal Annex Plus franchise."

_____

_____

_____

11. "I think I'll watch _Hour of Power_."

_____

_____

_____

12. "I'm going to volunteer for Bill Bradley's campaign."

_____

_____

_____

13. "I've decided to become a writer."

_____

_____

_____

14. "The gym has a one-week free trial. I'll take it."

_____

_____

_____

15. "Let's take that massage class."

_____

_____

_____

Brainstorming

The Skill:

Coming up with as many possible solutions as you can without pausing to evaluate them.

Exercise

You have determined various needs you and others might have in the last exercise. Now, brainstorm at least two alternative ways each of those needs might be fulfilled.

1. _____

   a. _____

   b. _____

2. _____

   a. _____

   b. _____

3. _____

   a. _____

   b. _____

4. _____

   a. _____

   b. _____

5. _____

   a. _____

   b. _____

6. _____

   a. _____

   b. _____

7. _____

   a. _____

   b. _____

8. _____

   a. _____

   b. _____

9. _____

   a. _____

   b. _____

10. _____

   a. _____

   b. _____

11. _____
   a. _____
   b. _____
12. _____
   a. _____
   b. _____
13. _____
   a. _____
   b. _____
14. _____
   a. _____
   b. _____
15. _____
   a. _____
   b. _____

Deciding On The Best Alternative

Exercise

Take a sheet of paper. For each of the needs above, write down the relative merits and shortcomings of each of the possible solutions you suggested. Then pick out which of the solutions you consider best and write out why.

Homework

Pick a personal problem you are interested in solving and use the Formula for Solving Problems presented on page 56 of *Lifeskills* to solve it. That is:

1. Identify the problem.
2. Decide to solve the problem.

3. Brainstorm possible solutions.
4. Decide on the best alternative.
5. Decide how to implement the plan.
6. Carry out the plan.
7. Hold a follow-up meeting.

7

Asking Others To Change Their Behavior

Making Observations, Not Assumptions

The Skill:

Describe what you saw the other person do or say, rather than your assumption about their motives. Telling others their motives frequently leads them to become so incensed that they will argue with you about the truth of your assumptions and never give another thought to your problem.

Tip: When you use this skill to fill in the "When . . ." portion of the "When . . . then" formula, it may help you to pretend you are simply a neutral observer reporting what you have seen.

Exercise

Turn the assumptions below into observations.

Example

"When you deliberately kept me waiting . . ."
"When you were 25 minutes late . . ."

1. "When you tried to win the argument by shouting . . ."

_____

_____

2. "When you purposely forgot my album . . ."

_____

_____

3. "When you tried to scare me into signing that agreement . . ."

_____

_____

4. "When you purposely embarrassed me by telling that joke . . ."

_____

_____

5. "When you knowingly betrayed me by telling my sister I lied . . ."

_____

_____

6. "When you intentionally misled me into thinking you were poor . . ."

_____

_____

7. "When you try to make me lose my cool . . ."

_____

_____

8. "When you tried to trick me into joining you in this 'invest-ment' . . ."

_____

_____

9. "When you pretended to be so knowledgeable about things you know nothing about . . ."

_____

_____

10. "When you show off in front of everybody . . ."

_____

_____

Exercise

Find a partner and have your partner write down everything you do as you role-play the following: Walk into the room and, without smiling or saying anything, slam the door shut. Hit your hand against the wall and go into another room, once again slamming the door. When you go over your partner's list, separate the observations from the assumptions and explain the difference to your partner. Next have your partner role-play some actions while you write down just your observations.

Completing Your Assertive Message

The Skill:

Completing the ". . . then" portion of the "When . . . then" formula by telling others the consequences of their behavior and perhaps how you feel about those consequences.

Example

When you were 25 minutes late, we missed the 4:30 bus.

Exercise

Complete each of the sentences above. Be sure once again not to make assumptions about others' motives as you describe the consequences of their behavior.

1. _____

_____

2. _____

_____

3. _____

_____

4. _____

_____

5. _____

_____

6. _____

_____

7. _____

_____

8. _____

_____

9. _____

_____

10. _____

_____

Delivering Direct Assertions

The Skill:

Delivering a statement that tells the other person exactly what change of behavior you want.

Exercise

Write out a direct assertion you could deliver to conclude each of the "When . . . then" statements above.

> ### Example
>
> When you were 25 minutes late, we missed the bus, so this time I want you to meet me promptly at 4:00.

1. _____

_____

2. _____

_____

3. _____

_____

4. _____

_____

5. _____

_____

6. _____

_____

7. _____

_____

8. _____

_____

9. _____

_____

10. _____

_____

Exercise

Pretend you want to ask others to change their behavior in each of the following situations. Write out a "When . . . then" statement, complete with a direct assertion. Practice delivering it to a friend.

1. A child is making too much noise.

_____

_____

_____

2. A salesman won't take no for an answer.

_____

_____

_____

3. A friend keeps calling after your bedtime.

_____

_____

_____

4. The driver of your car pool is going too fast.

_____

_____

_____

5. An acquaintance asks you questions you consider too personal.

_____

_____

_____

6. A doctor is using terms you don't understand to explain what's wrong with you.

_____

_____

_____

7. A friend has failed to return your calls.

_____

_____

_____

8. A co-worker whose advice you wanted stands you up for lunch.

_____

_____

_____

9. Your Step Study sponsor made a special point of urging you to attend this week and then didn't show up herself.

_____

_____

_____

10. A guest in your home takes out his pipe and begins to light up.

_____

_____

_____

11. A friend invites you to a seminar about an investment with "explosive" income potential, but won't tell you who's speaking or what type of investment will be discussed.

_____

_____

_____

12. A friend has invited you out to lunch. While you are waiting to be seated, he "discovers" that he has forgotten his wallet. He asks if you would mind lending him the money. This is the third time something like this has happened, and he has yet to pay you back.

_____

_____

_____

13. A close friend tells you she's angry at you but won't explain why.

_____

_____

_____

14. A friend refers to you as "cheap" — right in front of your family!

_____

_____

_____

15. A houseguest leans back and puts the dirty bottom of his shoes directly on your clean white wall.

_____

_____

_____

Homework

Write out three "When . . . then" statements you either could have used or can now use in your own life. Role-play delivering these statements with a partner playing the person whose behavior you want to change. Practice until you are happy with your performance.

1. _____

_____

_____

2. _____

_____

_____

_____

3. _____

_____

_____

If You Start To Panic

If you start to panic in doing this or any other exercise:

1. Stop the workout.
2. Sit down, take a few deep breaths, and relax.
3. Use a meditation tape or relaxation exercise if needed.
4. *Remember*
    a. This is only practice.
    b. You don't *have* to do anything with it in real life.

What tends to happen is that practice offers new ways of behaving. The more you practice, the more comfortable you will become with these new ways. Often you will then surprise yourself and begin using them without anxiety.

But you are under no obligation to do anything that makes you uncomfortable. Having new skills means having new choices. Choice means you can do what makes the most sense at the time. As you become more practiced, you may become less fearful and will then make different choices.

Learning a new skill does not mean you have to use it. It's perfectly okay for you to learn some of the skills in this book now and wait until another time when you feel more comfortable to begin using them.

8

Handling Criticism

Calling "Time Out" To Plan How
To Respond To Criticism

The Skill:

Declaring a halt in the action so you can prepare your response. Use it when you feel panicky in the face of criticism or are not sure of how to respond. Calling "Time Out" in a conversation is like calling "Time Out" in a basketball game. It gives you an opportunity to think quietly about what is being said, to calm down and to develop and practice your response.

Tip: If you find it difficult to ask for additional time, put a buffer sentence in between the criticism and your asking for time. Statements like "I'm sorry you feel that way," "I didn't know you felt that way," and "That was not my intent" let the other person know you heard the criticism. Further, they suggest that the criticism will be addressed at a later time.

Example

Sam: If you ask me, that idea of yours is crazy.
Your response: *I'd like to think about what you've said and get back to you later.*

Exercise

Write out a call for "Time Out" in each of the following situations.

1. Doug: That shirt looks terrible on you.

Your response: _____

_____

_____

2. Brad: That painting of yours is really . . . Well, it's ugly, is what it is.

Your response: _____

_____

_____

3. Frank: I've read that book and it's lousy.

Your response: _____

_____

_____

4. Shannon: I don't think much of your ACoA friends.

Your response: _____

_____

_____

5. George: You sent $50 to that television church?! What a sucker!

Your response: _____

_____

_____

6. Dan: Must you always be so emotional?

Your response: _____

_____

_____

7. Charlotte: Are you wearing that outfit *again?*

Your response: _____

_____

_____

8. Sandy: What a dumb comment you made. I feel embarrassed to be seen with you.

Your response: _____

_____

_____

9. Dick: How can you read the newspaper every day? It's so negative.

Your response: _____

_____

_____

10. Andrea: You need to have more fun. So stop working and let's go take in a movie.

Your response: _____

_____

_____

Vividly picture someone giving you each of the criticisms above while you respond to them with the words you have written out. Respond first in your mind and then out loud in front of a mirror. Be sure to

1. look directly at the other person,
2. speak calmly and matter-of-factly,
3. announce — don't ask — that you are going to take time out. Announcing gives *you* the power, while asking passes the power on to the other person.

Practice these exchanges with a friend. Ask your friend to tell you what you did well and how you could do even better. Practice some more, taking this feedback into account.

Exercise

Think of a situation in the past in which you were criticized and did a poor job of responding. Then imagine yourself re-writing history and calling "Time Out" in response to that criticism. You may find it helpful to write down your revised dialogue. How might you have done a better job of dealing with the criticism had you done that?

Homework

Practice calling "Time Out" in real life. Begin in unimportant situations and even in situations where there is no criticism. Perhaps a sales clerk asks if she can help you and you tell her you'll get back to her in a few minutes. Or perhaps a friend calls up and wants to talk and you tell her you'll call back soon. The important thing is to get used to responding when *you* are ready, rather than when someone else wants you to.

Requesting Specifics

The Skill:

Asking others exactly what it is that they don't like. Criticism is often given in generalities: "You don't look so good today," "You don't love me," "You didn't do a very good job." Adult children tend not to deal with criticism, hoping it will go away. More often than not it doesn't, and when you don't respond to

criticism, things generally only get worse. When you Request Specifics, you will understand the criticism. That is the first step toward dealing with it.

Tip: Maintain a neutral "I'm OK — You're OK" attitude. Act as though you're a reporter asking for the "Who? What? When? Where? Why? and How?" of a story. Most criticism is based on something you've done or haven't done, so focus on that. ("What did I *do* that made you say that?" is the question you'll ask most often.) You may also want to use active listening to indicate to the other person that they have been heard.

Example

Scott: You don't care for me.

Your response: *What have I done that makes you think I don't care for you?*

Exercise

Write out what you would say to Request Specifics in response to each of the following criticisms:

1. Mary: You're doing a lousy job.

Your response: _____

_____

_____

2. Doris: You're not a very good friend.

Your response: _____

_____

_____

3. Darlene: You don't look so good today.

Your response: _____

_____

_____

4. Bob: I don't like the way you acted last night.

Your response: _____

_____

_____

5. Marge: Why waste your time at those Adult Children meetings?

Your response: _____

_____

_____

6. Jack: Going back to school is a stupid idea.

Your response: _____

_____

_____

7. Don: You're not being very nice to me.

Your response: _____

_____

_____

8. Sarah: I'm not sure I like you hanging around that Dan. Can't you do better?

Your response: _____

_____

_____

9. Jim: You've graduated from college and you're still a waitress?

Your response: _____

_____

_____

10. Robert: This report you handed me is incomplete.

Your response: _____

Vividly picture yourself receiving each of these general criticisms above and calmly responding by Requesting Specifics using the words you have written above.

Practice several times delivering each of these responses in front of a mirror and while talking into a tape recorder. Each time strive to improve your delivery.

Have a friend give you each of these criticisms while you practice responding to them. Ask the friend to tell you what you did well and how you could do even better.

Homework

Whether they're being critical or not, when people you're with make general statements, practice Requesting Specifics. (Brad: "You really acted dumb last night." You: "What did I do that you think was dumb?")

Guess Specifics

The Skill:

Suggesting possible objections or criticisms. This skill will help your critics help you understand what they don't like when your Request for Specifics doesn't get you the details you want.

Tip: Once again maintain a calm, even voice, like a reporter seeking information.

Example

Scott: You don't love me anymore.
Your response: _What did I do that leads you to say that?_ (Requesting Specifics.)
Scott: I don't know.
Your response: _Is it the fact that I haven't kissed you today or yesterday?_
Scott: No, that's not it.
Your response: _Is it that I forgot to pack your lunch today?_
Scott: Yeah, and I went hungry all afternoon.

Exercise

Write out how you would respond to each of the following statements, beginning by Requesting Specifics and then, when you don't get any, by Guessing Specifics until you do get the answer.

1. Lisa: You're not a very good mommy.

Your response (Requesting Specifics): _____

_____

_____

Lisa: You know.

Your response: _____

_____

_____

Lisa: No, that's not it.

Your response: _____

_____

_____

Lisa: Yes, that's it!

2. Dana: You embarrassed me in front of everyone.

Your response (Requesting Specifics): _____

_____

_____

Dana: You know very well what you did.

Your response: _____

_____

_____

Dana: No, that's not it.

Your response: _____

_____

_____

Dana: No, although that wasn't very nice of you either.

Your response: _____

_____

_____

Dana: Yes, that's it.

3. Laura: You're wasting your time on that job.

Your response (Requesting Specifics): _____

_____

_____

Laura: I don't know. I just don't think there's a future in it.

Your response: _____

_____

_____

Laura: No.

Your response: _____

_____

_____

Laura: No.

Your response: _____

_____

_____

Laura: Yes, now you understand.

4. Dwight: I don't like that new friend of yours.

Your response (Requesting Specifics): _____

_____

_____

Dwight: I don't know. He just seems like a strange fellow.

Your response: _____

_____

_____

Dwight: Yeah, I guess that's it.

5. Boss: You're not doing a very good job here.

Your response (Requesting Specifics): _____

_____

_____

Boss: I'm not sure, but I know something's wrong.

Your response: _____

_____

_____

Boss: No.

Your response: _____

_____

_____

Boss: No, that's not it.

Your response: _____

_____

_____

Boss: You got it — that's it.

6. Larry: You don't seem all that happy today.

Your response (Requesting Specifics): _____

_____

_____

Larry: I'm just not sure.

Your response: _____

_____

_____

Larry: No, that's not it.

Your response: _____

_____

_____

Larry: Yeah, that's it.

Vividly picture yourself receiving each of the general criticisms above and then calmly responding using the words you have written to Request Specifics and then Guess Specifics.

Practice your responses several times in front of a mirror and while talking into a tape recorder. Each time, try to do better in some way.

Have a friend give you each of the criticisms above while you practice responding to them. Have your friend tell you first what you did well, and second how you could have done even better.

Exercise

Think of a situation in which you were criticized and didn't respond well. Change history by writing down the original criticism and then re-shaping the dialogue by using these skills.

Other: _____

_____

Your response: _____

_____

Other: _____

_____

Your response: _____

_____

Other: _____

_____

Your response: _____

_____

Homework

Whenever someone makes some vague criticism, Request Specifics. If you still don't get specifics, Guess Specifics until the other person agrees that you have guessed correctly. Congratulate yourself on your efforts.

Active Listening

The Skill (as it relates to handling criticism):

Reflecting back to the other person what the critical message means to you. Use this skill *when you are not certain you understood the criticism* and *when the criticism seems important or filled with emotion.*

Tip: Focus on the *content*, the *feelings* or both — depending on what you feel you may have misunderstood or what you think is most important. The other person will either confirm that you got it right or will correct your impression.

Example

Mandy: You embarrassed me in front of my mother.
Your response: _You sound angry._
Mandy: Yeah, calling me an Adult Child of an Alcoholic —
right in front of her!
Your response: _I insulted you when I said that._
Mandy: Not just _me!_ Not just _me!_ You insulted _both of us!_
Your response: _I embarrassed and wrongly attacked both you and your mother._
Mandy: Suppose I called you an Adult Child of Negative
Parents in front of _your_ parents?
Your response: _I wouldn't like it if you insulted my parents, and you don't like it that I insulted your mother._

Exercise

Write out how you would use Active Listening in response to
each of the following criticisms:

1. Ralph: How could you come out and tell my mother you're
an alcoholic?

Your response: _____

_____

_____

Ralph: Right. It just doesn't seem an appropriate response to
her offer of a drink.

Your response: _____

_____

_____

Ralph: Yes. It's fine that you are and I admire your licking this
problem, but I don't think you have to tell everyone.

Your response: _____

_____

_____

Ralph: Right. One thing more: I don't like having copies of *Sober Times* left all over the house. Do I have to be reminded of these problems ten times a day?

Your response: _____

_____

_____

Ralph: Right.

2. Lynn: You never pay any attention to me.

Your response: _____

_____

_____

Lynn: Yes, you promised our marriage counselor you'd take me out every other week, and the closest you've come is bringing home a video of *Police Academy 4*.

Your response: _____

_____

_____

Lynn: Right. Watching a video together doesn't count as a date. And anyway, you left halfway through to go do some work. How romantic!

Your response: _____

_____

_____

3. Donna: Next time Ronnie stays over at your house, please don't let him stay up so late.

Your response: _____

_____

_____

Donna: Right. He came home *so* tired, I put him right to bed. Wouldn't let him go to school.

Your response: _____

_____

_____

Donna: Yes. And he had sand in his hair and his clothes were all dirty.

Your response: _____

_____

_____

Donna: Right. I'm glad to see you understand.

Agree With The Truth

The Skill:

Acknowledging when criticism you are given is in fact accurate. When criticism is true, your most powerful response is to agree with it. Most of the time you're simply acknowledging the truth of criticism to satisfy your critic and end the criticism. You may well gain some new insights from using this skill.

Tip: Agree in an "I'm OK — You're OK" manner. You may have made a mistake, but you're still OK. Doing so will make it far more likely that others will respond to you with respect and without jumping all over you. Also, if you plan on doing anything about the criticism, say so, as that will further satisfy your critics.

Example

John: You still haven't cleaned up the garage.
Your response: *That's true. I'm just getting ready to do it.*

Exercise

Write out how you would Agree With the Truth in responding to each of the following situations.

1. Nate: You're late.

Your response: _____

_____

_____

2. Patricia: Your report isn't finished.

Your response: _____

_____

_____

3. Tom: You haven't touched your broccoli.

Your response: _____

_____

_____

4. Jerry: Your library book is overdue.

Your response: _____

_____

_____

5. Marge: You haven't phoned John in over two months!

Your response: _____

_____

_____

6. John: You've been reading for two hours, and you're still just on page 20?

Your response: _____

_____

_____

7. Ian: Our phone bill shows $23 in daytime calls. If you phoned after five or before eight, we'd save a bundle.

Your response: _____

_____

_____

8. Cynthia: Haven't seen you at the last two Weight Watchers meetings.

Your response: _____

_____

_____

9. Melanie: You've spent a week on that project already!

Your response: _____

_____

_____

10. Dick: Your shoes are dirty.

Your response: _____

_____

_____

11. Randi: You could have spent more time preparing your talk.

Your response: _____

_____

_____

12. Bob: Your car is sort of small.

Your response: _____

_____

_____

13. Elliot: You sounded like you had a touch of stage fright up there.

Your response: _____

_____

_____

14. Susan: I got a raise to $300 a week. That's $50 more than you.

Your response: _____

_____

_____

15. Jean: That pen of yours leaked and got ink all over my pants!

Your response: _____

_____

_____

Vividly picture yourself receiving each of the criticisms above and calmly and confidently responding to them using the words you have written out.

Practice responding to each of these criticisms while speaking in front of a mirror and talking into a tape recorder. Ask yourself: "Did I stand up straight?" "Did I look confident?" "Did I make good eye contact with where the other person would be?" "Did I talk too softly? Too loud?" "Did I sound OK or not OK?" "Was my voice flat — or lively?" Taking the feedback you give yourself into account, repeat this exercise until you are happy with your delivery.

Have a friend give you each of the criticisms above while you practice responding to them. Ask your friend to tell you what he or she thinks you did well and how you could have done better.

Homework

When people you're with make critical statements — whether they're being critical of you or not — practice Agreeing With the Truth. (Gina: "Houses in California cost three times as much as houses in Florida. That's crazy!" You: "I agree, it doesn't make any sense to me either.") Compliment yourself whenever you do this well, and forget about times when you don't.

Agreeing With The Odds

The Skill:

Acknowledging that your critics *may* be right. Since no one can be certain of the future, you can agree that things *may* work out their way while still holding on to your position.

Tip: To *really* leave your critics feeling understood, back up their opinions with even more evidence.

Example

Mona: If you leave school, you'll never go back.
Your response: *You may be right. Plenty of people who leave school never do return. But I want to take a year off to travel and have fun. And I'm sure that if I set my mind to it, I will go back.*

Exercise

Write out how you would Agree With the Odds in responding to each of the following comments.

1. Marsha: If you keep driving that motorcycle, you're going to have an accident.

Your response: _____

_____

_____

Marsha: And when you do, you're probably going to get pretty banged up.

Your response: _____

_____

_____

Marsha: If your head got hit, it would crack like an egg.

Your response: _____

_____

_____

2. Randy: If you don't save more, you're going to wind up in the poorhouse.

Your response: _____

_____

_____

3. Kent: If you don't work harder, you'll lose your job.

Your response: _____

_____

_____

4. Alice: If you don't go along with Ralph, he won't want to be your friend.

Your response: _____

_____

_____

5. Donna: Stop being so particular! If you don't find a husband soon, you probably never will.

Your response: _____

_____

_____

6. Todd: If you keep eating like that, you're gonna get fat.

Your response: _____

_____

_____

7. Dean: If you'd study more, you'd get better grades.

Your response: _____

_____

_____

8. Bob: If you stay home, you'll miss a good time.

Your response: _____

_____

_____

9. Sam: If you aren't nicer to the teacher, he's going to flunk you.

Your response: _____

_____

_____

10. Dora: If you keep watching so much television, your brain will turn to mush.

Your response: _____

_____

_____

11. Lynn: If you don't get a house soon, you'll never be able to get one. Prices are going right up to the sky!

Your response: _____

_____

_____

12. Salesman: This offer is the chance of a lifetime. An opportunity like this will *never* come again!

Your response: _____

_____

_____

13. Sandra: Don't bother inviting Joe. He wouldn't want to come anyway.

Your response: _____

_____

_____

14. Bev: No use your going on a diet. Nobody *ever* sticks to a diet!

Your response: _____

_____

_____

15. Dawn: A blind date? I wouldn't waste my time if I were you. I've been on lots of blind dates, and I never met a man I really liked.

Your response: _____

_____

_____

Vividly picture yourself receiving each of the criticisms above and calmly and confidently responding to them with the words you have written out.

Practice delivering the lines you have written out while looking into a mirror and talking into a tape recorder. Critique yourself and practice again and again until you are satisfied with your delivery.

Have a friend give you each of the criticisms above while you practice responding to them. Ask your friend to tell you what he or she thinks you did well and how you could do even better.

Homework

Whether they're criticizing *you* or not, when people you're with make statements about the odds, practice Agreeing With the Odds. (Lana: "I think the meeting will be full." You: "I agree. With ten people here already, it's likely a lot more people will show up.")

Disagree With The Criticism

The Skill:

Rejecting criticism and voicing an opposing viewpoint. It's okay to simply say, "I disagree," and then say why.

Tips: Be especially wary of criticism that includes the word "should." ("You should spend more time reading history if you want to understand what's going on today.") "Should" statements tend to be moralistic in tone and to mask the fact that what is said is merely someone else's opinion. When criticism is vague, don't forget to Ask for Specifics before responding.

Example

Amy: It's ten 'clock already and you haven't done a bit of work.

You: *I disagree. I've made three phone calls and written one report.*

Exercise

Write out how you would Disagree with the Criticism in response to each of the following statements:

1. Rod: I think you should have fired Jim when you found him stealing stamps.

Your response: _____

_____

_____

2. Jim: Those brown shoes don't match your pants at all.

Your response: _____

_____

_____

3. Rosemarie: You should look for a new job if they won't give you a dental plan.

Your response: _____

_____

_____

4. Stan: Your garage is so messy, I don't know how you can stand it. I think you should spend all day Saturday cleaning it up.

Your response: _____

_____

_____

5. Doris: That blouse really doesn't become you. You should take it back.

Your response: _____

_____

_____

6. Theresa: You stay home too much. Tonight you should kick up your heels and go dancing!

Your response: _____

_____

_____

7. Richard: You really should subscribe to the newspaper. How else will you be well informed?

Your response: _____

_____

_____

8. Esther: Your clothes do look good on you, but they're out of style.

Your response: _____

_____

_____

Clearly picture yourself receiving each of these criticisms and calmly and confidently disagreeing with them using the words you have written out.

Practice responding to each of the criticisms above using the words you have written out while looking in a mirror and talking into a tape recorder. Critique yourself several times and each time practice doing better.

Have a friend role-play giving you each of these criticisms while you practice responding to them. Ask your friend to tell you what you did well and how you could do better.

Exercise

Think back to a time when you were being criticized, a time you wish you had used this skill. Write out the criticism and how you wish you had responded here:

Other: _____

_____

Your Response: _____

_____

Homework

When people you meet are critical — even if they are not being critical of you — practice Disagreeing with the Criticism and voicing your own opinion. (Other: "Roger would be better off quitting his job." You: "I disagree. Since he doesn't know what he wants to do, I think he's better off staying where he is.")

Agree With The Critic's Right To Differ

The Skill:

Acknowledging that your critic has a valid opinion, while asserting that you don't accept it or intend to change your behavior.

Tips: Consider beginning your response with *"I can see how you might think that . . ."* Your critic will especially like it if you state some reasons why his point is reasonable. And then state your own opinion and intention. Keep your "I'm OK — You're OK" stance. Neither of you is right or wrong; you're just two people who disagree.

Example

Roger: How can you read the *Enquirer?* That is the dumbest newspaper in the world!

You: *I can see how you might think that. The* Enquirer *can be pretty dumb. But I enjoy reading it now and then.*

Exercise

Write out how you would Agree with the Critic's Right to Differ in response to each of the following statements:

1. Adele: Why are you wasting your life doing such uncreative work? Someone like you should be an artist or a writer.

Your response: _____

_____

_____

2. Susan: ACoA, AA, NA. Can't you just get well on your own?

Your response: _____

_____

3. Jean: Club Med *sounds* like a good place for you to spend your vacation. But after a few days it gets boring.

Your response: _____

_____

_____

4. Lorraine: How can you go sailing the Caribbean with some second-rate line? Don't you know Royal Cruise Lines offers by far the best value?

Your response: _____

_____

_____

5. Art: I don't see how you can be such good friends with George. All he talks about is money.

Your response: _____

_____

_____

6. Lynda: You can't be serious about buying junk bonds. Don't you know that market is down for good?

Your response: _____

_____

_____

7. Chad: Writing things out won't work. There's only one way to get rid of anger — scream!

Your response: _____

_____

_____

8. Ted: You ought to quit sales and go into banking. It's much more steady and secure.

Your response: _____

_____

_____

9. Dirk: Reading *Calvin and Hobbes* at your age? When are you going to grow up?

Your response: _____

_____

_____

10. Mary: I think you should go for Dave, the rich one. Rick may treat you nicer, but Dave . . . well, he's got all that money!

Your response: _____

_____

_____

11. Ray: You shouldn't let your past trouble you. Hey, today is a new day and the sun is shining!

Your response: _____

_____

_____

12. Marcia: Get the Lincoln. If you really had faith in yourself, you wouldn't worry about making enough to pay it off.

Your response: _____

_____

_____

13. James: If you're not sure what you want to do with your life, go back to school. You'll find the answers there.

Your response: _____

_____

_____

14. Henry: If you haven't got over your problems by now, you're never going to.

Your response: _____

_____

_____

15. Andy: This city is too expensive. I think you should go out to the country where land is cheap.

Your response: _____

_____

_____

Vividly picture yourself receiving each of the criticisms above and confidently answering each of them with the words you've written above.

Practice delivering each of your responses while facing a mirror and talking into a tape recorder. Repeat the process until you are happy with your delivery.

Have a friend give you each of these criticisms while you practice responding to them. Ask your friend to tell you first what
you did well and then what you could have done better. Practice
until you are satisfied you have done as well as you can.

Homework

When you disagree with criticism, whether it's of you or not,
practice Agreeing with Your Critic's Right to Differ. Begin with
"I can see how you might think that . . ." and give the other
person some evidence to back up his or her point. Then state
your own point of view. Don't forget to praise yourself for whatever part of this or any other exercise you do well and to give
yourself some reward.

9

Establishing And
Defending Boundaries

How To Know When You Need Boundaries

The Skill:

Setting up and maintaining barriers between you and other people, limitations beyond which you will not go and beyond which others are not welcome.

Exercise

Make a list of the 10 most important relationships in your life. (List your relationship with your boss as one of these, whether or not you consider it that important.)

1. _____
2. _____
3. _____

4. _____

5. _____

6. _____

7. _____

8. _____

9. _____

10. _____

If you are well-connected with your feelings, as you interact with these people over the next few days or weeks, write down next to their names the various feelings you experience.

Example

3. _My Boss_ — _happy/angry/upset/sad/very mad/happy_

If you find you feel angry, depressed, beaten down, used, violated, overworked or any combination of these, it is a warning sign that you need to establish boundaries.

Next, examine these relationships in terms of what you give to them and what you get from them. (Not what you *are going* to get or what you *hope* to get, but what you really *do* get right now, this week, *today*.) Take 10 pieces of paper and put the name of one of these people on top of each. Draw a line down the center of each page and put *cost* on the left column and **reward** on the right column. Then fill in the columns.

Example

Marsha's "friend" Matt

Cost	Reward
I spend $30 or more a week feeding him.	He tells me he loves me.
I baby-sit his bratty child.	I feel needed.
I run errands for him.	I'm not so lonely.
I listen to his problems.	I enjoy his company — when he's sober.
I drive him home when he calls me and he's drunk.	
I take his verbal abuse.	
He's hit me twice, and I'm afraid he will again.	

Good healthy relationships are a fair exchange. The costs to you are about equal to the rewards. (Keep in mind, however, that the value you place on any cost or reward is subjective — you alone determine it. For example, if you have to drive 10 miles on the freeway to help someone, that may or may not be a significant cost, depending on how you feel about driving.) Adult Children often give far more than they get and aren't even aware of the imbalance. When you examine your relationships this way, you can tell whether you are giving about as much as you are getting. If you aren't, *you need boundaries.*

Do this exercise even if you already know your exchanges are lopsided and even if you already know you are not ready to do anything about them. It will help you to get ready. If you act before you are ready, you may not be able to stick with what you say or be able to handle the response. Take whatever time you need and don't judge yourself harshly if you are not ready yet.

Setting Personal Boundaries

The Skill:

Deciding what boundaries are appropriate for you and announcing them.

The best time to set boundaries is before they are needed. That way you'll have plenty of time to figure out what boundaries you want and what you will do if someone tries to violate them.

In the relationships above in which you have determined that you need boundaries, ask yourself what boundaries would be best.

Ask friends who appear to have good relationships what boundaries they think you should set and what boundaries they would set for themselves. Ask yourself what boundaries you would recommend if someone you love were in your situation. Then decide to love yourself and set up those very same boundaries.

Exercise

On one or more clean sheets of paper write out your new boundaries. Put those sheets of paper up on a mirror, in a desk or somewhere else where you will see them often. Take the process seriously. Remember, you need boundaries to maintain your integrity as a human being. If your boundaries are to mean anything, you must decide to stick to them *no matter what*.

Example

If you were Marsha and involved with Matt in the example above, you might set the following boundaries:

I will not feed him when he comes over unannounced.

I will not baby-sit his child except when the child is already in bed.

I will not talk to him when he calls me and is drunk.

I will not allow him — or anyone else — to verbally abuse me.

I will not allow him — or anyone else — to hit me.

Having set your boundaries, you will need to announce them if they are to have an impact on your life. In some cases, as with Marsha's decision not to baby-sit anymore, you can wait until the situation arises before announcing your boundaries. In other cases, like Marsha's decision that she will not allow anyone to verbally abuse or hit her, you are best off announcing your boundaries in advance.

Exercise

Decide which of your new boundaries you need to announce in advance.

Imagine yourself announcing your boundaries and having the other person agree not to violate your boundaries anymore.

Practice announcing your boundaries in front of a mirror and into a tape recorder and then with a partner. Continue practicing until your tone of voice and your body language convey the seriousness of your purpose. Consider using "If . . . then" contingencies (discussed later in this chapter) to announce your boundaries.

Example

Marsha: Matt, I'm upset about your hitting me and verbally abusing me during our fight last week. I've been working to set up boundaries, and I have decided I will never allow that to happen again.
(and, using "If . . . then" contingencies)
Marsha: If you ever hit me in the future, I will call the police and press charges. Further, if you hit me or verbally abuse me again, I will never see you again.

Sometimes you will need to set boundaries on the spot. Your response should be brief, to the point, and at least part of it should be suitable for using as a Broken Record statement if need be.

Exercise

Write out what you would say to set boundaries in each of these situations:

1. At the mall, an attractive fellow with a clipboard asks you to take five minutes to answer some questions.

Your response: _____

_____

_____

2. A salesman knocks on your door while you are working. You may be interested in what he is selling, but you don't want to take a break now.

Your response: _____

_____

_____

3. A friend asks you to give blood, and you decide you don't want to.

Your response: _____

_____

_____

4. You have been waiting for a parking space. When it finally opens up, another driver steals it.

Your response: _____

_____

_____

5. A good friend urges you to sign up with his multi-level vitamin company — only $250 to start!

Your response: _____

_____

_____

6. A fellow worker invites you to explore what you consider a dangerous part of town.

Your response: _____

_____

_____

7. Your neighbor invites you to attend his church's worship service next Sunday.

Your response: _____

_____

_____

8. A friend invites you to join him in a real estate investment. "A sure thing!" he says.

Your response: _____

_____

_____

9. A business associate invites you to co-host (and pay for!) an expensive banquet.

Your response: _____

_____

_____

10. You were looking forward to a quiet weekend, but then a friend calls up to ask if he can get your opinion on a problem of his.

Your response: _____

_____

_____

Changing And Defending Personal Boundaries

The Skill:

Announcing new personal boundaries and protecting them. Suppose you have had other boundaries in the past. Are you bound to them forever? Absolutely not! You can change them, *just because you say so*, even if you don't have a good reason. If your new boundaries are challenged — and they will be — simply Agree with the Truth, Agree with the Odds, Disagree, and Agree with the Critic's Right to Differ and then re-assert your new boundary using Broken Record.

Tip: Be prepared for the fact that this change will not be well received. You will be changing the rules, and the chances are those you are addressing will not be willing participants in this change. Why should they be? If you have been willing to meet their needs under the old rules, this shift will be disconcerting at least and will provoke anger or rejection at most. Knowing this ahead of time will be useful. That way you will not be surprised by the initial reaction. But among those who really care about you, the second reaction will be an understanding of your position and maybe even a grudging admiration.

> **Example**
>
> Jack: Marla, will you please type up these papers. They're important.
> Marla: I'll be happy to type them until six, but I've decided not to work past six anymore.
> Jack: But you worked until nine just last week. Come on!
> Marla: That's true. In the past I used to work late, but I've decided not to work after six anymore (Agrees with the Truth and Broken Record).

Exercise

Write out what you would say to change your boundaries in each of the following situations:

1. You've quit smoking yourself, and now you've decided not to allow anyone else to smoke in your home. Your neighbor Fran is just about to light up.

You say: _____

_____

_____

Fran: You never told me that before.

You say: _____

_____

_____

Fran: In fact, you and I used to light up together. Nothing like a nice smooth smoke after dinner.

You say: _____

_____

_____

2. Your brother Ricky has asked you to lend him $600 to help him make his mortgage payments. Following some bad experiences, you and your mate have decided not to loan anyone money ever again.

You say: _____

_____

_____

Ricky: You can't really mean it.

You say: _____

_____

_____

Ricky: But you lent me $1,000 last year when I had those gambling debts. And I paid you off, didn't I?

You say: _____

_____

_____

Ricky: I even paid you interest, didn't I?

You say: _____

_____

_____

Ricky: If I don't get this money, they'll foreclose on my house.

You say: _____

_____

_____

Ricky: And even if they don't take it away, it'll still cost me thousands in attorney's fees.

You say: _____

_____

_____

Ricky: Come on! I'm your brother!

You say: _____

_____

_____

3. Laura: I know you've got your ACoA meeting, but why don't you skip it this time and stay for dinner?

You say: _____

_____

_____

Laura: But you've skipped your meeting in the past for a good home-cooked meal. What's one more time?

You say: _____

_____

_____

Laura: Come on, they never say anything really new at those meetings anyway.

You say: _____

_____

_____

4. Your sister has stayed with you over Christmas the past four years. Each year her unkind remarks have left you feeling lonely and depressed and you promised yourself never to invite her back for the holidays. Now she's calling to tell you when she'll arrive this year.

You say: _____

_____

_____

Sister: But you can't do that. I *always* come for the holidays.

You say: _____

_____

_____

Sister: You can't just decide to change things. My visit is a family tradition.

You say: _____

_____

_____

Sister: But now that Mom's died, I'm all the family you've got.

You say: _____

_____

_____

Sister: If I don't come, you'll be terribly lonely over the holidays.

You say: _____

_____

_____

One of the most common situations in which Adult Children need to change their boundaries is at work, where they have been doing favors for co-workers and are forever being asked to do more. If this is a problem for you, the strategies above will work. Additional strategies you might use which are suggested by Rick Potter, a therapist in Costa Mesa, California, include:

1. Announcing, when you see people you normally do favors for, that you are very busy. This will make it less likely they will ask you for anything.
2. Asking *them* for favors. This will *convince* them you're too busy!
3. Agreeing to help, but explaining that you'll only have time in a week. They probably won't want to wait that long and will do it themselves.

Exercise

Role-play with a partner using each of these strategies with co-workers. Each time you do it, take any constructive criticism your partner may give you into account and do it again.

Calling "Time Out" To Plan
How To Defend Your Boundaries

The Skill:

Asking for more time to decide if your boundaries are threatened or to decide how to defend them. When you feel a need to call "Time Out," say matter-of-factly, "I'm not ready to answer. I'll call you back _____." You can promise to reply in an hour, a day, a week — whatever seems right for you.

Example

Andy: Can I borrow 20 bucks till Tuesday?
Your response: *I'm not ready to answer. I'll call you back on this tomorrow.*

Exercise

Write out a call for "Time Out" in each of the following situations:

1. Becky: Mind if I make a toll call to my Uncle George? It's his birthday and he'd be upset if I didn't call.

Your response: _____

_____

_____

2. Carole: What a terrific shirt! Can I borrow it for the weekend?

Your response: _____

_____

_____

3. Donna: I know you've got studying to do this weekend, but a bunch of us are watching *Teenage Mutant Ninja Turtles* tonight. How about joining us?

Your response: _____

_____

_____

4. Sid: I know we're over budget, but can I please get those pants anyhow?

Your response: _____

_____

_____

5. Mike: Will you take care of my dogs the week I'm gone? They've only got a few fleas — no biggie . . . I wouldn't trust anyone but you to watch them.

Your response: _____

_____

_____

6. Helen: You're got a lot of extra room here. Mind if I store some extra furniture in your garage for a while?

Your response: _____

_____

_____

7. Frank: Is it okay if Marge and I house-sit for you while you're away?

Your response: _____

_____

_____

8. Your boss: Would you mind coming in Saturday? I've got a project for you.

Your response: _____

_____

_____

9. Harv: Can I borrow your car to pick up my uncle at the airport?

Your response: _____

_____

_____

10. Lynn: How about a nice big kiss?

Your response: _____

_____

_____

Deliver An Assertive "No!"

The Skill:

Turning away attempts to cross your boundaries by delivering an assertive "No."

Tips: To deliver an assertive *no*, be sure to:

1. Stand up straight.
2. Make eye contact.
3. Speak clearly and firmly.

Exercise

Practice saying *"No"* to each of the following requests. Do not add any other comments. Just say *"No."* Talk into a tape recorder at first. Then practice with a partner. If you are a woman, make a special effort to find a male partner. Women often say "no" in ways that men interpret as meaning "Yes" or "Maybe" or as being seductive. So specifically ask your partner for feedback on this and for help in delivering a "No" that *will* be taken seriously.

1. Would you mind coming over and looking at my plant? I can't figure out why it's dying.
2. Say, can I borrow that book?

3. Can I take a moment of your time and tell you about a great investment opportunity?
4. I thought I'd just drop by and shoot the breeze. May I come in?
5. Our ball's on your roof. Do you mind if I climb up and get it?
6. I'm here collecting for the Retired Fishermen's Fund. How much would you like to donate?
7. May I use your computer tonight? I broke mine.
8. You have such a lovely house. Would you mind terribly if we got married here?
9. Can I leave the girls with you while I give a speech? They have colds, but I'm sure you wouldn't catch anything.
10. I have a problem that's troubled me for years. May I come by and tell you all about it?
11. Since your child is such a good student, I know you won't mind if we switch him to a new class we're forming.
12. I'm going door to door collecting for the United Way in my neighborhood. Will you volunteer to do the same in yours?
13. I happen to be in the neighborhood. Mind if I drop by?
14. I know you have a rule against taking work home, but will you please do it just this one time?
15. I know you asked me not to call after ten, but I need your advice about my new guy. Can we talk?

Broken Record

The Skill:

Repeating a short refusal statement over and over again.

Tip: Many people think they have to invent a different excuse each time someone asks for something. You don't. You can simply wait them out by repeating the same refusal statement over and over again in the same calm tone of voice.

Exercise

Vividly picture yourself replying to Madge by saying "No" over and over again, no matter what she says and no matter how long she says it. Then do the same out loud in front of a mirror and into a tape recorder. As you evaluate your delivery ask yourself, "Is this *No* going to be taken seriously?" Then practice some more until you are sure that it will be.

1. Madge: Would you baby-sit for Erick tonight?

Your response: _____

_____

_____

Madge: I know this is short notice, but I'd sure appreciate it.

Your response: _____

_____

_____

Madge: But Erick especially asked for you.

Your response: _____

_____

_____

Madge: And you know how he doesn't like strangers to baby-sit. If you say no, we'll have to get a stranger.

Your response: _____

_____

_____

Madge: Look, we'll pay you. Will $2 an hour do?

Your response: _____

_____

_____

Madge: Okay, $3 an hour.

Your response: _____

_____

_____

Madge: You would really be helping me out of a jam.

Your response: _____

_____

_____

Madge: I've already paid for these concert tickets, and if you won't baby-sit we won't be able to go, and I'll lose the money I spent.

Your response: _____

_____

_____

Madge: You know, you're playing awfully hard to get.

Your response: _____

_____

_____

Madge: When you've needed help, haven't I been there? Like when you needed me to pick up that table you bought at the garage sale. Didn't I help?

Your response: _____

_____

_____

Madge: And when you needed to use my phone, didn't I let you?

Your response: _____

_____

_____

Madge: So please baby-sit for Erick. Neighbors should help each other.

Your response: _____

_____

_____

Go through this same dialogue and instead of saying "No," substitute a refusal statement and say it over and over again. You might, for example, have as your refusal statement, "I've got to go to the office," "I already have plans," or "I want to be alone tonight." Practice both with a tape recorder and with a partner. Ask yourself and your partner what you did well and how you could have done better. Then practice some more until you are pleased with your delivery.

Go through the same dialogue, only this time before repeating your refusal statement, use the skills of Active Listening, Agreeing with the Truth, Agreeing with the Odds, Disagreeing, and Agreeing with the Critic's Right to Differ to deal with the other person's objections. Write out your responses first. Then practice calmly and matter-of-factly delivering them into a tape recorder and to a partner.

For more practice, go through steps one, two and three above with the following dialogues:

2. Dennis: Say, my aunt's flying in and I wonder if I could borrow your car to pick her up?

Your response: _____

_____

_____

Dennis: It would really impress her. My car's just an old clunker.

Your response: _____

_____

_____

Dennis: I'd only want it for an hour or two. Then you could have it the whole afternoon.

Your response: _____

_____

_____

Dennis: You know, this isn't the first time you've loaned me your car.

Your response: _____

_____

_____

Dennis: The last time, I returned it safe and sound. I even filled it up with gas and cleaned the windows.

Your response: _____

_____

_____

Dennis: You know, I'm not asking for anything I haven't done for you. You've borrowed my car a time or two.

Your response: _____

_____

_____

Dennis: Well, now it's your turn to help me. Friends gotta help friends.

Your response: _____

_____

_____

Dennis: Look, I told my aunt I'm doing well. What's she gonna think if I pull up in a 1981 Datsun 210?

Your response: _____

_____

_____

Dennis: Well, if I can't have the car for the airport, can I at least borrow it Saturday to take her to the ball game?

Your response: _____

_____

_____

3. Lynn: You know, we've been dating for two weeks now, and I think it's time we went to bed.

Your response: _____

_____

_____

Lynn: Two weeks is the longest I've waited for anyone. I want you so much!

Your response: _____

_____

_____

Lynn: You know you can't expect to keep a romantic relationship going if you don't, you know, come across.

Your response: _____

_____

_____

Lynn: But it's only natural. Two people who feel like we do _should_ get together.

Your response: _____

_____

_____

Lynn: I'm coming to deeply care about you, and it's just human for me to want to express that love.

Your response: _____

_____

_____

Lynn: Perhaps you aren't attracted to me. Perhaps that's it. (Sob)

Your response: _____

_____

_____

Lynn: I brought a condom, if that's what's troubling you.

Your response: _____

_____

_____

Lynn: Okay, reject me if you want, but you'll only have yourself to blame if I go off and find somebody else.

Your response: _____

_____

_____

4. Gary: Can you lend me $20 'til payday?

Your response: _____

_____

_____

Gary: But I could really use it. I'm taking Susie out this weekend and I want to show her a good time.

Your response: _____

_____

_____

Gary: You know, I wouldn't ask if I didn't need it.

Your response: _____

_____

_____

Gary: If you don't lend me the money, I'll have to rent some boring movie. You wouldn't want me to have to do that, would you?

Your response: _____

_____

_____

Gary: Hey, aren't we friends? Aren't friends supposed to help each other?

Your response: _____

_____

_____

Gary: You know, if you needed a loan and I had the money, I'd lend it to you.

Your response: _____

_____

_____

Gary: Okay, how about ten bucks? Aren't I good for ten bucks?

Your response: _____

_____

_____

Gary: Five bucks?

Your response: _____

_____

_____

Gary: *Two* bucks?

Your response: _____

_____

_____

Gary: It doesn't sound like you're gonna help me out.

Your response: _____

_____

_____

Homework

If you are typical, you will find no shortage of occasions to use these skills in your daily life. (One of the co-authors of this book counted an average of seven occasions *a day!*) Go out of your way to practice them. When salesmen call, instead of hanging up, use the Broken Record technique when they try to close the sale. One student of ours even spent time at a used car dealer's showroom, a masochistic — but rigorous — way to practice!

"If . . . Then" Contingencies

The Skill:

Telling others what you will do if they continue to violate your boundaries. Simply fill in the blanks of the following formula: "If you continue _____, then I'm going to _____."

Example

A salesman keeps asking you to buy and won't take no for an answer.

Your response: *If you continue asking me to buy, then I'm going to hang up.*

Exercise

Write out how you would use "If . . . then" Contingencies in the following situations:

1. A neighbor's dog keeps you up at night. "What can I do?" she says. "My dog is lonely."

You say: If you continue _____

then I'm going to _____

_____

2. An old friend keeps bringing up your ex, even after you've asked her to stop. "Someone like J.J., you'll never find again," she says.

You say: _____

_____

_____

3. A friend you have been casually dating starts kissing you.

You say: _____

_____

_____

4. You told a neighbor's eight-year-old daughter not to put her muddy fingerprints on your white walls, and she didn't listen. Now she's walking in and getting ready to do it again.

You say: _____

_____

_____

5. A friend keeps judging you for going to ACoA meetings. "If you believed in yourself, you wouldn't have to go to those meetings," she says.

You say: _____

_____

_____

6. For the past year you've been politely asking a girlfriend to take back her books which are stored in your garage. She has promised to take them "soon."

You say: _____

_____

_____

7. Your mate hits you.

You say: _____

_____

_____

8. Your fellow keeps bragging about old girlfriends.

You say: _____

_____

_____

9. Your ex has the children every weekend and always brings them back an hour or more late.

You say: _____

_____

_____

10. Your ex fails to make child support payments.

You say: _____

_____

_____

11. A used car dealer says he'll give you a great price on a Chevy but only if you agree to buy today.

You say: _____

_____

_____

12. An acquaintance says you are welcome to join her social group *if* you also join her vitamin multi-level marketing group.

You say: _____

_____

_____

13. You and your mate have promised to follow the rules for fighting fair. Now the two of you are in a fight, and your mate keeps calling you "dumb" and "crazy."

You say: _____

_____

_____

14. You loaned your car to Roger once and he returned it two hours late. Now you've loaned it again, he agreed to have it back by ten, and he's phoning to say he's having such a good time he won't have it back 'til morning!

You say: _____

_____

_____

15. You've gone home for the holidays, and your aunt keeps talking about embarrassing mistakes you made in the past.

You say: _____

Imagine yourself reciting each of the "If . . . then" Contingencies you wrote above and getting a positive response from the other person.

Pretend you're in each of the situations above. First, practice while facing a mirror and then while talking into a tape recorder. Next, with a friend, practice saying each of the comments you have written out. Each time critique yourself and have your friend tell you what you did well and how you could do better. Continue practicing until you are satisfied.

Homework

Use this skill in real life whenever you find your boundaries being violated. But be sure you are prepared to act on the "then" part of the contingency before announcing it. If you aren't, those who violate your boundaries may very well sense it. And if you don't follow through, they won't take you seriously next time.

10

Fighting Fair

Homework

Buy a piece of white cardboard at least two feet by three feet large. Use a felt-tipped pen to write out the Do's and Don'ts of fighting fair that appear in Chapter Ten of *Lifeskills*. You needn't write out every word, just the key words that appear in italics. Post this sign in a room where you and others will see it often. That way when you have a fight and someone breaks a rule, others can easily point that out. Agree on a punishment for breaking a rule, like the loss of part of an allowance or a fine.

Exercise

Find a partner and pick a topic about which neither of you is highly emotional. Practice having a fight while following the "Procedural Rules" for fighting fair in Chapter Ten of *Lifeskills* and following the Do's and Don'ts written on the sign. Point out to each other when you fail to follow either of these, and practice doing better. Congratulate yourself for whatever success you have and give yourself a reward.

11

Ending Conversations And Visits

Ending Conversations

The Skill:

Making it clear to your conversational partner that you wish to conclude the interaction.

Exercise

Practice delivering each of the following statements while talking into a tape recorder. As you listen back, ask yourself: "Did I talk too softly? Too loudly?" "Did I sound okay or not okay?" "Did I sound serious about ending the conversation?" Practice over and over until you are satisfied with your delivery.

"Excuse me for just a moment."
"Excuse me, but I have to go now."
"I have to get back to work. Talk to you another time."
"I'm going to get a bite to eat. 'Bye."

"Excuse me, but I see my aunt. I'm going to go say hello. 'Bye."
"I've enjoyed talking with you. 'Bye for now."
"I have to go pick up my son. 'Bye."
"Thanks for your help, Jack. 'Bye."
"I appreciate your taking the time to give me your thoughts. 'Bye."
"I'll think about your idea and call you next Tuesday."
"I'm looking forward to our brainstorming session Tuesday."
"I hope to see you here again."
"Let's exchange phone numbers so we can talk some more about this."

Practice delivering each of these comments while facing a mirror. Ask yourself if your facial expressions and the rest of your body language are congruent with your message. Adjust your delivery accordingly as you repeat this exercise until you are satisfied with the nonverbal aspects of your delivery.

Exercise

With a friend, pretend that you have been in a conversation for a while and are ready to leave. As you continue talking, practice giving each of the following nonverbal cues that you intend to end your conversation.

Put your jacket on.
Talk slower or faster.
Give your voice a higher or lower pitch.
Respond less, both verbally and nonverbally.
Move toward the door as you walk.
Move away from the other person in circles that get larger and larger as you talk.

Each time ask your friend to tell you what you did well and how you could do even better. Try again until you and your friend agree that you have done it in a way that effectively conveys your message.

Exercise

Practice by yourself and with your friend, first giving each of your nonverbal cues and then supplementing it with your verbal cues.

12

Ending Relationships

Coming To A Decision

Skill #1:

Objectively listing what you *give* and what you *get* in a relationship to see if there is a fair exchange taking place. Many Adult Children spend years in thoroughly unsatisfying relationships because they think things are always about to work out, because the other person says he loves them or because they enjoy giving so much they almost feel as though they are getting. Satisfying relationships are based on fair exchanges. Listing what you give and what you get will help you get in touch with what the costs and rewards of your relationships really are.

Example

What I Give	*What I Get*
My apartment. I pay the rent.	He contributes some money when I'm short.
I cook almost every night.	He makes special dinners now and then.
The use of my car.	The use of his car when mine is in the shop.
Companionship.	I'm not alone.
I clean the house.	
I buy the food.	
I pick him up when he's drunk.	
Love.	Good sex.

Exercise

Analyze one of your relationships in this way, especially one you are thinking of leaving. Be sure to list only things you and the other person are *actually contributing*, not things you think you will get someday.

Skill #2:

Objectively listing the pros and cons of leaving the relationship. It is not a good idea to come to conclusions about breaking up amidst the chaos of arguing, threatening, begging and promises to do better. You will do better by quietly sitting down and listing the pros and cons of leaving. Looking over your lists, you'll find the right decision for you will often become obvious.

Example

Pros Of Leaving	Cons Of Leaving
I won't be hit anymore.	He is good to me (when he's sober).
I won't have to deal with his drunken insults and attacks.	He is a good father (when he's sober).
I can save some money — I won't have to pay his bills anymore.	He keeps me company.
I won't have to wait around bars to take him home.	
My children won't have his bad example around.	
I'll be free to find a man who treats me well.	

Exercise

List the pros and cons of leaving one of your relationships. Once again, don't list promises or wishes of how you hope things will be. Just list things *as they actually are*. Sometimes the decision will be obvious, but other times the pros and cons will be fairly evenly balanced. Sometimes there will be lots of cons — reasons why you ought to stay — but only a few very compelling pros like, "He beats me" or "He abuses our son." If this is the case for you, give extra weight to these and we urge you to consult a counselor if you are still in doubt. Most problems do not go away, and not deciding is the same as deciding to stay.

Ending Unimportant Relationships

The Skill:

If you have decided to leave an unimportant relationship, consider leaving it right away. Simply:

1. Do not call the other person.
2. Screen your calls with an answering machine and do not answer this person's calls.
3. Do not return calls.
4. If the other person does make contact with you, answer all invitations by saying, "Sorry, I'm too busy." If it's important to you to be totally frank, say, "I'd rather not see you again." If the other person persists, use either remark as your Broken Record statement.

Tip: Don't bother giving lots of excuses or going into depth on why the other person is "bad" or "wrong." You have chosen to end the relationship for reasons that make sense to you and that is enough. Don't pretend you plan to get together in the future when you don't. That will only encourage some people to try again and again.

Example

Thom: Let's get together for lunch Saturday.
You: *Sorry, I'm too busy.*
Thom: How about lunch a week from Saturday?
You: *Sorry, I'm too busy.*

Exercise

With a friend acting out the part below, practice saying, "Sorry, I'm too busy" or "I'd rather not see you again" over and over. Be sure to use the same flat tone of voice each time as you recite your Broken Record, and maybe even sound a little bored.

Brent: How about taking in the races next Saturday?

Your response: _____

_____

Brent: Come on, we'll have fun!

Your response: _____

_____

Brent: I'll drive.

Your response: _____

_____

Brent: I'll even pay for your admission.

Your response: _____

_____

Brent: Come on, I'd like to take you out.

Your response: _____

_____

Brent: I know you don't want to go cause you're low on cash. Look, I'll lend you $20 or $30.

Your response: _____

_____

Brent: All right, I'll *give* you $10.

Your response: _____

_____

Tip: You don't *have* to go on and on responding as long as the other person talks. You can end the process simply by saying, "Sorry, but I've got to go," and then hanging up or leaving.

Ending Important Relationships

Before deciding to leave an important relationship, consider using the lifeskills in our accompanying book. You may be able to turn your relationship around by using them.

If you have decided to leave the relationship, consider doing so immediately. Leaving won't be any easier next week or next year, and why waste more of your time in a relationship that simply has no future? You can phone or simply write a note. If you decide to meet the other person face to face, consider the following advice.

Asking To Meet In A Public Place

The Skill:

Issuing an invitation to meet at a restaurant, a park or another location where lots of people will be around. If the other person tries to talk you into changing your plans, either agree to meet at another public place at another time or use Broken Record. Violence or screaming are far less likely in a public place than in your home, so whatever you do, *do not give in*.

Exercise

With a friend, practice issuing the following invitation and then using Broken Record to stick with it.

You say: I've something important to tell you, and I'd like to meet you at Denny's tomorrow morning at eight o'clock.

Rick: Why don't you just come here?

You say: _____

_____

Rick: I tell you what. I'll drive by tonight.

You say: _____

_____

Rick: Well, why don't you just tell me now?

_____

_____

_____

Rick: Okay, 8 A.M. tomorrow at Denny's it is.

Deliver Your Message

Remember to be brief, to stick to the present, to begin your feeling messages with "I" and to make it clear that you are ending the relationship. Consult *Lifeskills* for specifics. It normally helps to plan your statement in advance, so you can be sure you say everything you intend to say and also so you can practice in advance.

Exercise

On a sheet of paper, write out a sample statement announcing the end of your relationship. Practice reciting that statement in front of a mirror and into a tape recorder until you feel you have done a satisfactory job of delivering it.

It is unlikely that someone with whom you have had an important relationship will simply nod, accept what you have to say and leave. More likely the response will be to give you reasons why you should change your mind and to promise to do better. When you practiced ending an unimportant relationship, it was enough for you simply to use Broken Record. When ending an important relationship with someone you have cared about, you may wish to also use the skills of Active Listening, Agreeing with the Truth, Agreeing with the Odds, and Agreeing with the Critic's Right to Differ.

Exercise

Use the skills in parentheses to write your response to each of the following statements:

You: This isn't easy for me to say but . . . I've changed and I've decided not to go on seeing you.

Don: Hey, I know I haven't treated you so well lately, but I'll do better.

You (Active Listening):_____

_____

_____

Don: Right. I'll be much better to you.

You (Agree with the Truth and Broken Record): _____

_____

_____

Don: You sound serious. But I remember the last time you broke up, you changed your mind. (He smiles).

You (Agree with the Truth and Broken Record): _____

_____

_____

Don: So I think you'll take me back again. At least I hope you will.

You (Agree with the Critic's Right to Differ and Broken Record):

_____

_____

_____

Don: Look, what do you want? How about a nice dinner to make it up to you?

You (Active Listening): _____

_____

_____

Don: Yes, I think so. Look, I love you. Or at least I think I *could* love you.

You (Agree with the Truth and Broken Record): _____

_____

_____

Don: Okay, you got me in the dog house. How long are you gonna keep me there?

_____

_____

Don: Well, isn't that why you're giving me a hard time?

You (Agree with the Critic's Right to Differ and Broken Record):

_____

_____

_____

Don: You're gonna miss me.

You (Agree with the Odds and Broken Record): _____

_____

Don: You won't find someone else like me.

You (Agree with the Odds and Broken Record): _____

_____

_____

Don: Isn't there anything I can do to get back with you?

You (Broken Record): _____

_____

_____

Exercising skills is just like exercising muscles. First you learn what is appropriate. Then you practice. At first it hurts like hell but if you stay with it and make it part of your daily routine you will reap the benefits. We wish you well.

Janet Woititz
Alan Garner

About The Author

Janet Geringer Woititz, Ed.D., is the founder and President of the Institute for Counseling and Training in West Caldwell, New Jersey, which specializes in working with dysfunctional families and individuals. She is the author of the best-selling *Adult Children Of Alcoholics* and *Struggle For Intimacy* as well as *Marriage On The Rocks, Healing Your Sexual Self, The Self-Sabotage Syndrome: Adult Children In The Workplace* and *Lifeskills for Adult Children* with Alan Garner. Her books are also available as tapes.

Alan Garner, M.A., is a nationally known relationship-skills trainer who lives in Laguna Hills, California. He is the author of *A Search For Meaning, Conversationally Speaking, Lifeskills for Adult Children* with Janet G. Woititz and the million-selling parent/child manual *It's OK to Say No to Drugs!*

Other Books by Janet G. Woititz

Adult Children Of Alcoholics (Expanded Edition)

There are some 28 million children of alcoholics living in the United States. This heritage has followed all of them into adulthood. What they need is basic information to sort out the effects of alcoholism in their lives. Dr. Woititz's book is the first to provide this crucial material.

ISBN 1-55874-112-7   (Soft cover 5½x8½ 130 pg.)
Code 1127 .... $8.95

Marriage On The Rocks

What is a wife to do when "he" drinks too much? . . . When the marriage is "on the rocks?" Sensitive, thoughtful, compassionate advice is offered for the wife living with and loving an alcoholic husband. The time for change is now . . . the tools for change are here.

ISBN 0-932194-17-6   (Soft cover 5½x8½ 147 pg.)
Code 4176 .... $6.95

Struggle For Intimacy

This book is must reading for everyone wanting more from their intimate relationships with spouses, lovers, friends and family. The "struggle" doesn't have to be quite so tough . . . and this book will show you how to get what you want from your relationships.

ISBN 0-932194-25-7   (Soft cover 5½x8½ 101 pg.)
Code 4257 .... $6.95

Healing Your Sexual Self

How can you break through the aftermath of sexual abuse and enter into healthy relationships? In this book, Dr. Woititz explains in clear and direct language that the process begins with recognizing that *something has gone wrong* and how to deal with your recovery.

ISBN 1-55874-018-X   (Soft cover 5½x8½ 138 pg.)
Code 018X $7.95

Lifeskills For Adult Children
With Alan Garner

Imagine how good you would feel if you could stand up for yourself without losing your temper or make a decision without second-guessing yourself. *Lifeskills For Adult Children* teaches these and other interpersonal skills that can make your life easier while improving your sense of self-worth.

ISBN 1-55874-070-8   (Soft cover 5½x8½ 160 pg.)
Code 0708 .... $8.95

The Self-Sabotage Syndrome

Adult Children are among any company's most productive employees but if you are an Adult Child, you may be treading too close to workaholism, burnout and other problems on the job. Janet Woititz describes what signs indicate trouble on the job and how to make your work more satisfying.

ISBN 1-55874-050-3   (Soft cover 5½x8½ 144 pg.)
Code 0503 .... $8.95

New Books . . .
from Health Communications

ALTERNATIVE PATHWAYS TO HEALING: The Recovery Medicine Wheel
Kip Coggins, MSW
This book with its unique approach to recovery explains the concept of the
medicine wheel — and how you can learn to live in harmony with yourself,
with others and with the earth.
ISBN 1-55874-089-9 $7.95

UNDERSTANDING CO-DEPENDENCY
Sharon Wegscheider-Cruse, M.A., and Joseph R. Cruse, M.D.
The authors give us a basic understanding of co-dependency that everyone
can use — what it is, how it happens, who is affected by it and what can
be done for them.
ISBN 1-55874-077-5 $7.95

THE OTHER SIDE OF THE FAMILY:
A Book For Recovery From Abuse, Incest And Neglect
Ellen Ratner, Ed.M.
This workbook addresses the issues of the survivor — self-esteem, feelings,
defenses, grieving, relationships and sexuality — and goes beyond to help
them through the healing process.
ISBN 1-55874-110-0 $13.95

OVERCOMING PERFECTIONISM:
The Key To A Balanced Recovery
Ann W. Smith, M.S.
This book offers practical hints, together with a few lighthearted ones, as a
guide toward learning to "live in the middle." It invites you to let go of your
superhuman syndrome and find a balanced recovery.
ISBN 1-55874-111-9 $8.95

LEARNING TO SAY NO:
Establishing Healthy Boundaries
Carla Wills-Brandon, M.A.
If you grew up in a dysfunctional family, establishing boundaries is a
difficult and risky decision. Where do you draw the line? Learn to recognize
yourself as an individual who has the power to say no.
ISBN 1-55874-087-2 $8.95

3201 S.W. 15th Street,
Deerfield Beach, FL 33442
1-800-851-9100

**Health
Communications, Inc.**

Other Books By . . .
Health Communications

ADULT CHILDREN OF ALCOHOLICS
Janet Woititz
Over a year on *The New York Times* Best-Seller list, this book is the primer on Adult Children of Alcoholics.
ISBN 0-932194-15-X   **$6.95**

STRUGGLE FOR INTIMACY
Janet Woititz
Another best-seller, this book gives insightful advice on learning to love more fully.
ISBN 0-932194-25-7   **$6.95**

BRADSHAW ON: THE FAMILY: A Revolutionary Way of Self-Discovery
John Bradshaw
The host of the nationally televised series of the same name shows us how families can be healed and individuals can realize full potential.
ISBN 0-932194-54-0   **$9.95**

HEALING THE SHAME THAT BINDS YOU
John Bradshaw
This important book shows how toxic shame is the core problem in our compulsions and offers new techniques of recovery vital to all of us.
ISBN 0-932194-86-9   **$9.95**

HEALING THE CHILD WITHIN: Discovery and Recovery for
Adult Children of Dysfunctional Families — Charles Whitfield, M.D.
Dr. Whitfield defines, describes and discovers how we can reach our Child Within to heal and nurture our woundedness.
ISBN 0-932194-40-0   **$8.95**

A GIFT TO MYSELF: A Personal Guide To Healing My Child Within
Charles L. Whitfield, M.D.
Dr. Whitfield provides practical guidelines and methods to work through the pain and confusion of being an Adult Child of a dysfunctional family.
ISBN 1-55874-042-2   **$11.95**

HEALING TOGETHER: A Guide To Intimacy And Recovery For
Co-dependent Couples — Wayne Kritsberg, M.A.
This is a practical book that tells the reader why he or she gets into dysfunctional and painful relationships, and then gives a concrete course of action on how to move the relationship toward health.
ISBN 1-55784-053-8   **$8.95**

3201 S.W. 15th Street,
Deerfield Beach, FL 33442-8190
1-800-851-9100

Health
Communications, Inc.

Daily Affirmation Books from . . .
Health Communications

GENTLE REMINDERS FOR CO-DEPENDENTS: Daily Affirmations
Mitzi Chandler

With insight and humor, Mitzi Chandler takes the co-dependent and the adult child through the year. Gentle Reminders is for those in recovery who seek to enjoy the miracle each day brings.

ISBN 1-55874-020-1   **$6.95**

TIME FOR JOY: Daily Affirmations
Ruth Fishel

With quotations, thoughts and healing energizing affirmations these daily messages address the fears and imperfections of being human, guiding us through self-acceptance to a tangible peace and the place within where there is *time for joy.*

ISBN 0-932194-82-6   **$6.95**

AFFIRMATIONS FOR THE INNER CHILD
Rokelle Lerner

This book contains powerful messages and helpful suggestions aimed at adults who have unfinished childhood issues. By reading it daily we can end the cycle of suffering and move from pain into recovery.

ISBN 1-55874-045-6   **$6.95**

DAILY AFFIRMATIONS: For Adult Children of Alcoholics
Rokelle Lerner

Affirmations are a way to discover personal awareness, growth and spiritual potential, and self-regard. Reading this book gives us an opportunity to nurture ourselves, learn who we are and what we want to become.

ISBN 0-932194-47-3
(Little Red Book)   **$6.95**
(New Cover Edition)   **$6.95**

SOOTHING MOMENTS: Daily Meditations For Fast-Track Living
Bryan E. Robinson, Ph.D.

This is designed for those leading fast-paced and high-pressured lives who need time out each day to bring self-renewal, joy and serenity into their lives.

ISBN 1-55874-075-9   **$6.95**

3201 S.W. 15th Street,
Deerfield Beach, FL 33442-8190
1-800-851-9100

Health
Communications, Inc.